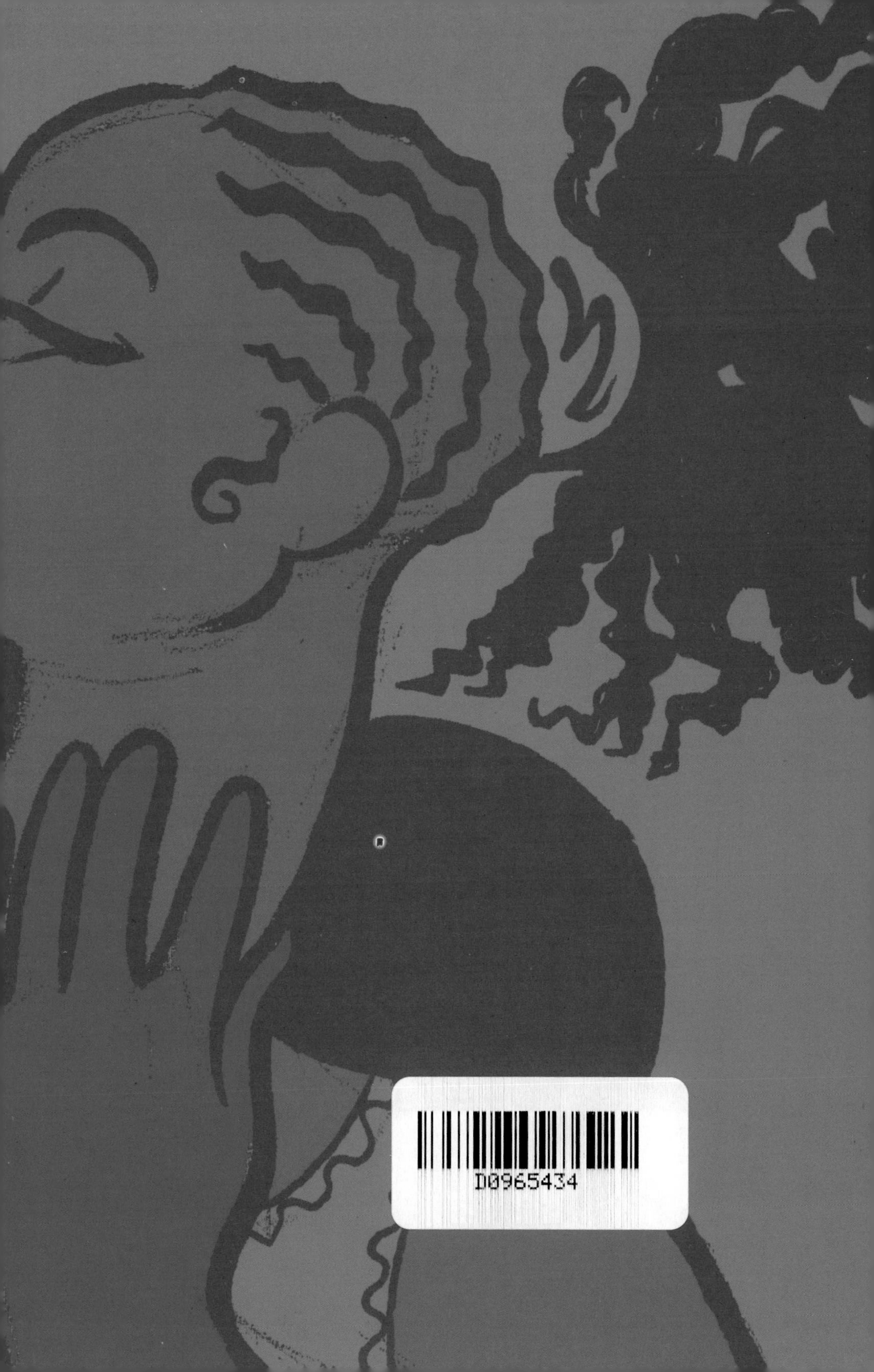

LUCIFER'S GARDEN OF VERSES

2 —

LUCIFER'S GARDEN OF VERSES
VOLUME ONE

the Devil on Fever Street

Lance Tooks

ISBN 1-56163-409-3 hc
ISBN 1-56163-412-3 pb
© 2004 Lance Tooks
printed in Singapore

3   2   1

Library of Congress Cataloging-in-Publication Data

Tooks, Lance.
    Lucifer's garden of verses / Lance Tooks.
        p. cm.
    Contents: v. 1. The Devil on Fever Street
    ISBN 1-56163-409-3 (v. 1: cloth : alk. paper) -- ISBN 1-56163-412-3 (v. 1: pbk. : alk.
paper)
        I. Title.

    PN6727.T664L83 2004

                                                                                    2004049999

ComicsLit is an imprint
and trademark of

ComicsLit

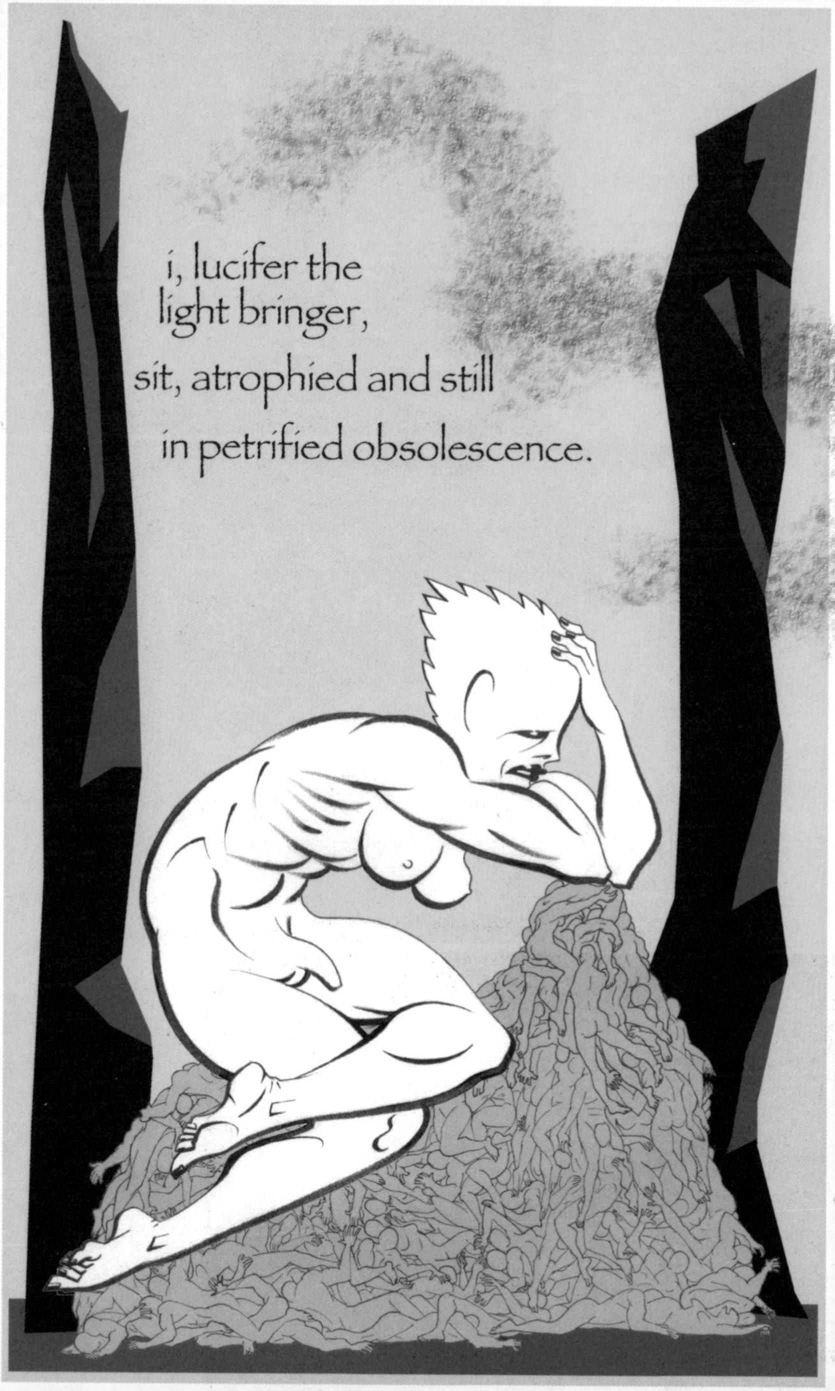
i, lucifer the
light bringer,
sit, atrophied and still
in petrified obsolescence.

blameless, i,
for the state of
your world,
a devil's relevance
and power for
near a century,
dwarfed by the
greedy evasions
of man

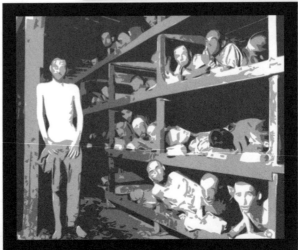

pinched
tween a
mighty
thumb &
forefinger,
mere pawns
in a game
are you
and i

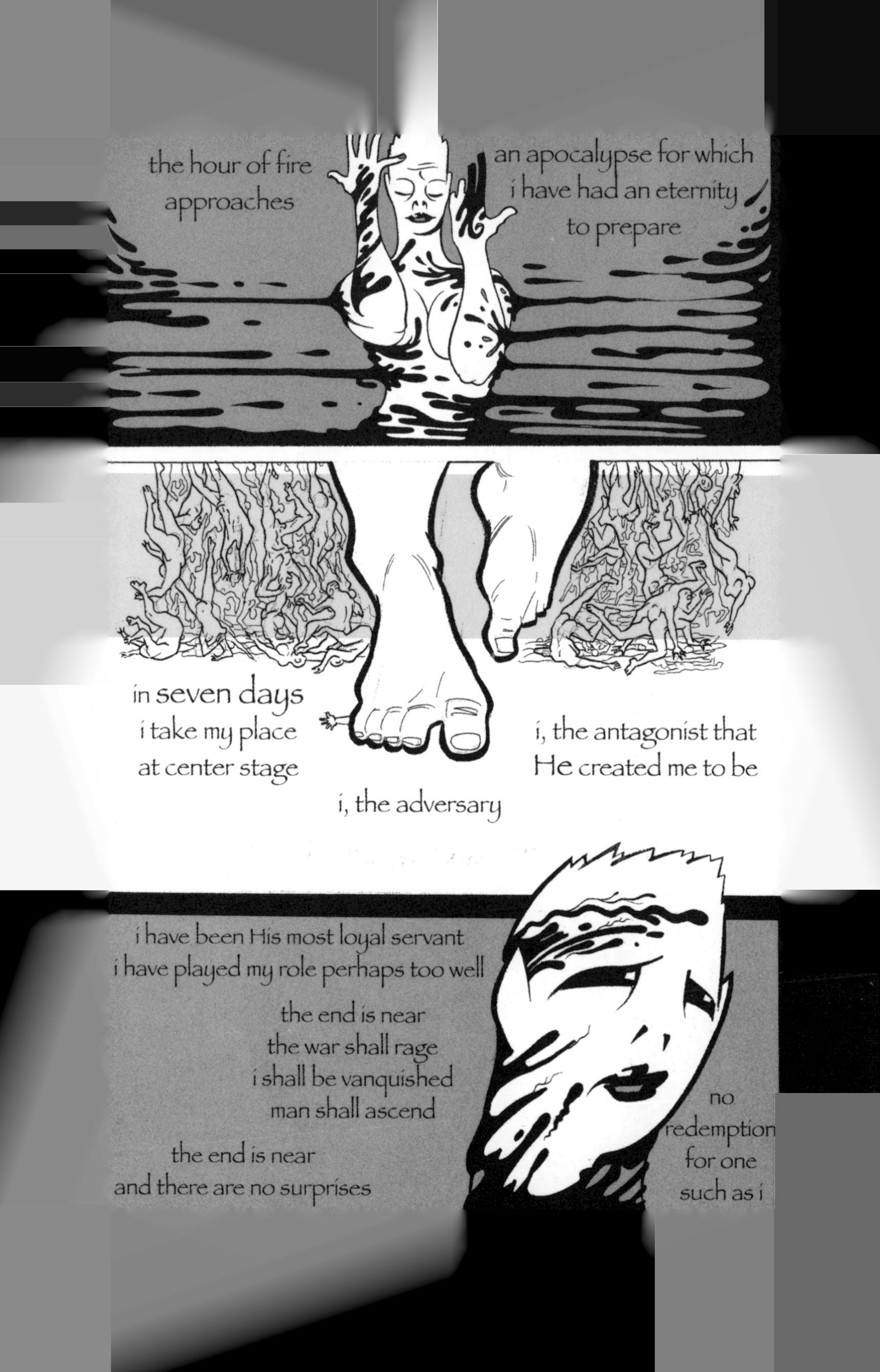
the hour of fire
approaches
an apocalypse for which
i have had an eternity
to prepare
in seven days
i take my place
at center stage
i, the adversary
i, the antagonist that
He created me to be
i have been His most loyal servant
i have played my role perhaps too well
the end is near
the war shall rage
i shall be vanquished
man shall ascend
the end is near
and there are no surprises
no
redemption
for one
such as i

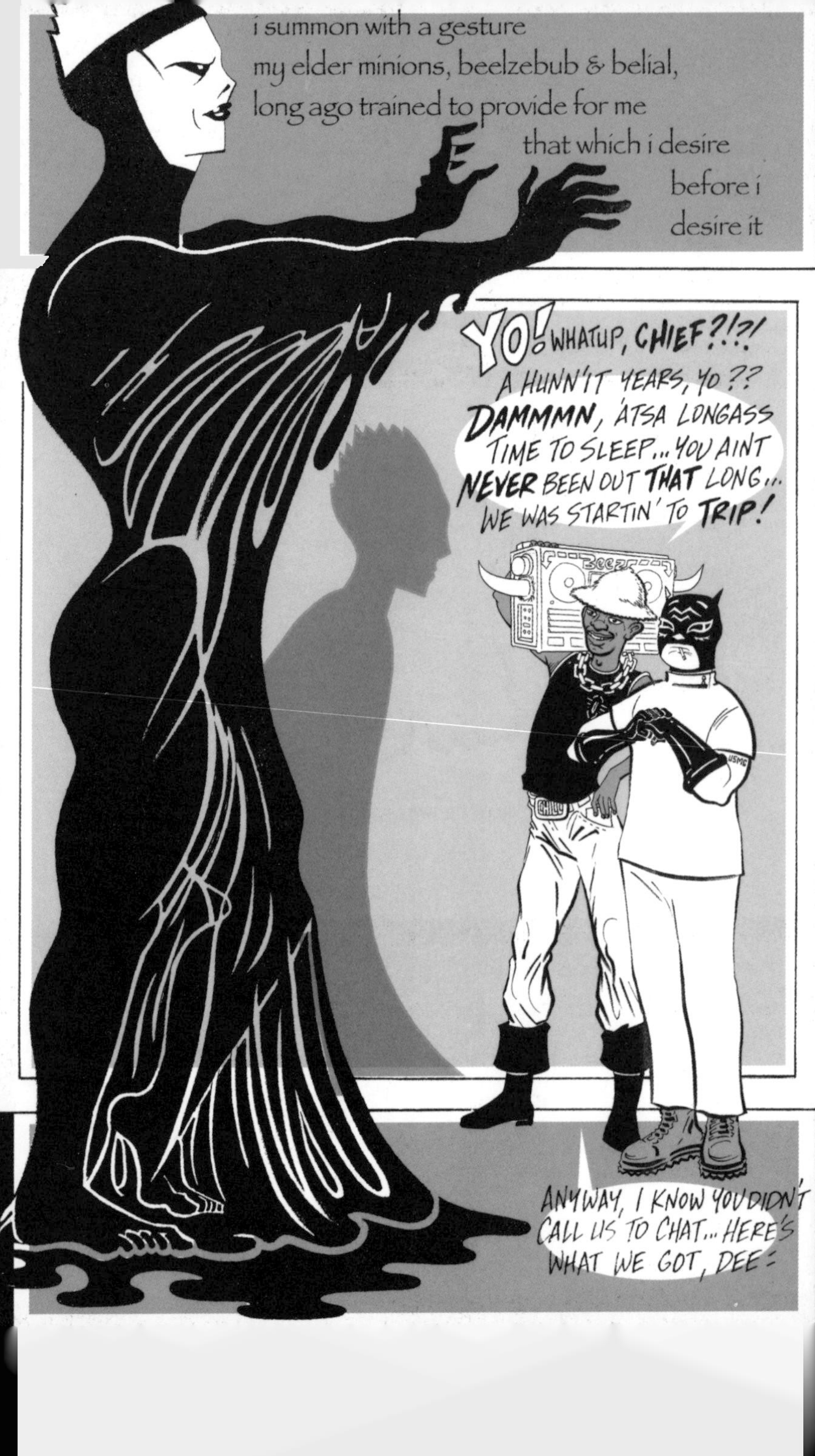
i summon with a gesture
my elder minions, beelzebub & belial,
long ago trained to provide for me
that which i desire
before i
desire it
YO! WHATUP, CHIEF?!?! A HUNN'IT YEARS, YO?? DAMMMN, 'ATSA LONGASS TIME TO SLEEP... YOU AINT NEVER BEEN OUT THAT LONG... WE WAS STARTIN' TO TRIP!
ANYWAY, I KNOW YOU DIDN'T CALL US TO CHAT... HERE'S WHAT WE GOT, DEE:

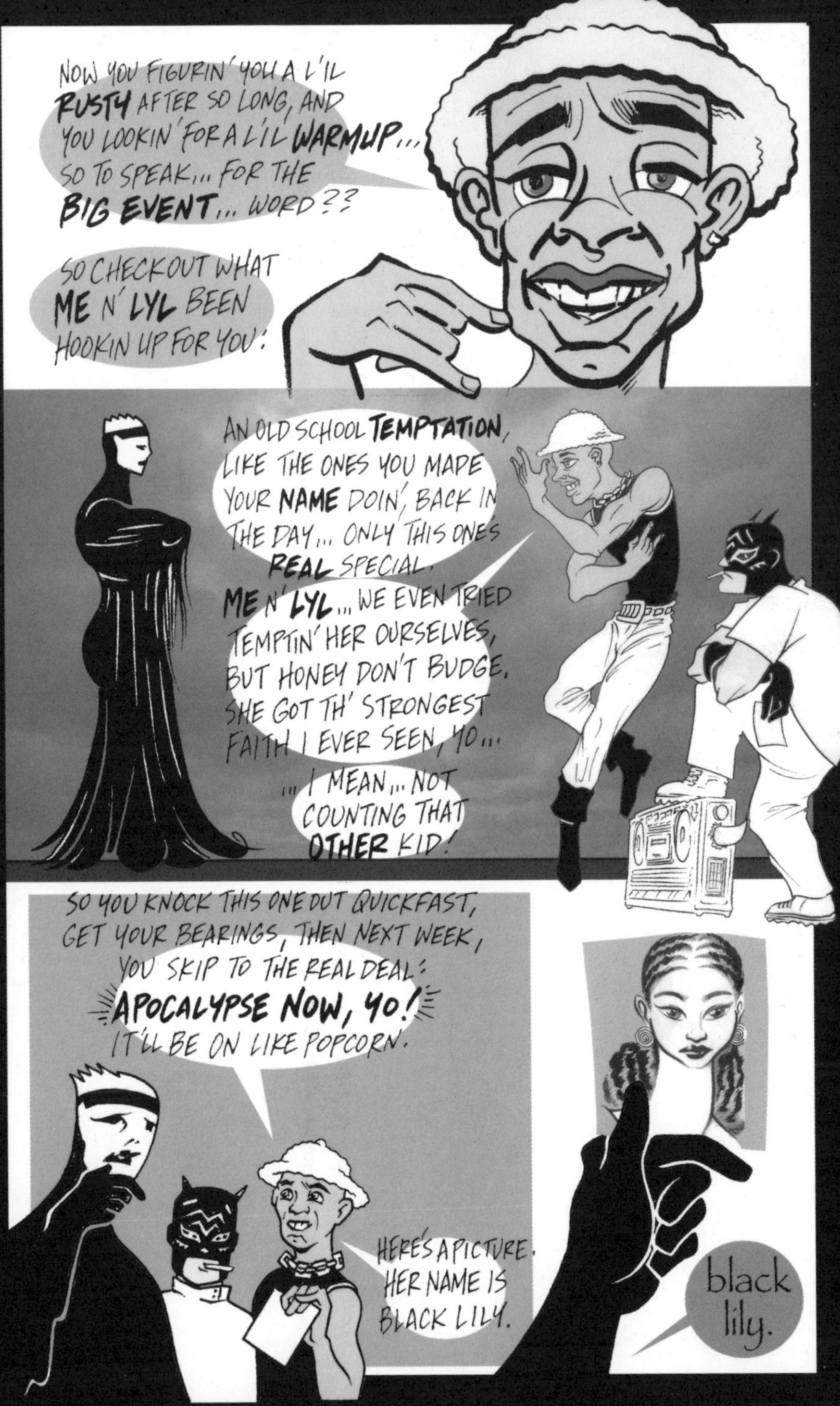
NOW YOU FIGURIN' YOU A L'IL RUSTY AFTER SO LONG, AND YOU LOOKIN' FOR A L'IL WARMUP... SO TO SPEAK... FOR THE BIG EVENT... WORD??
SO CHECKOUT WHAT ME N' LYL BEEN HOOKIN UP FOR YOU:
AN OLD SCHOOL TEMPTATION, LIKE THE ONES YOU MADE YOUR NAME DOIN', BACK IN THE DAY... ONLY THIS ONE'S REAL SPECIAL.
ME N' LYL... WE EVEN TRIED TEMPTIN' HER OURSELVES, BUT HONEY DON'T BUDGE. SHE GOT TH' STRONGEST FAITH I EVER SEEN, YO...
...I MEAN... NOT COUNTING THAT OTHER KID!
SO YOU KNOCK THIS ONE OUT QUICKFAST, GET YOUR BEARINGS, THEN NEXT WEEK, YOU SKIP TO THE REAL DEAL: APOCALYPSE NOW, YO! IT'LL BE ON LIKE POPCORN.
HERE'S A PICTURE. HER NAME IS BLACK LILY.
black lily.

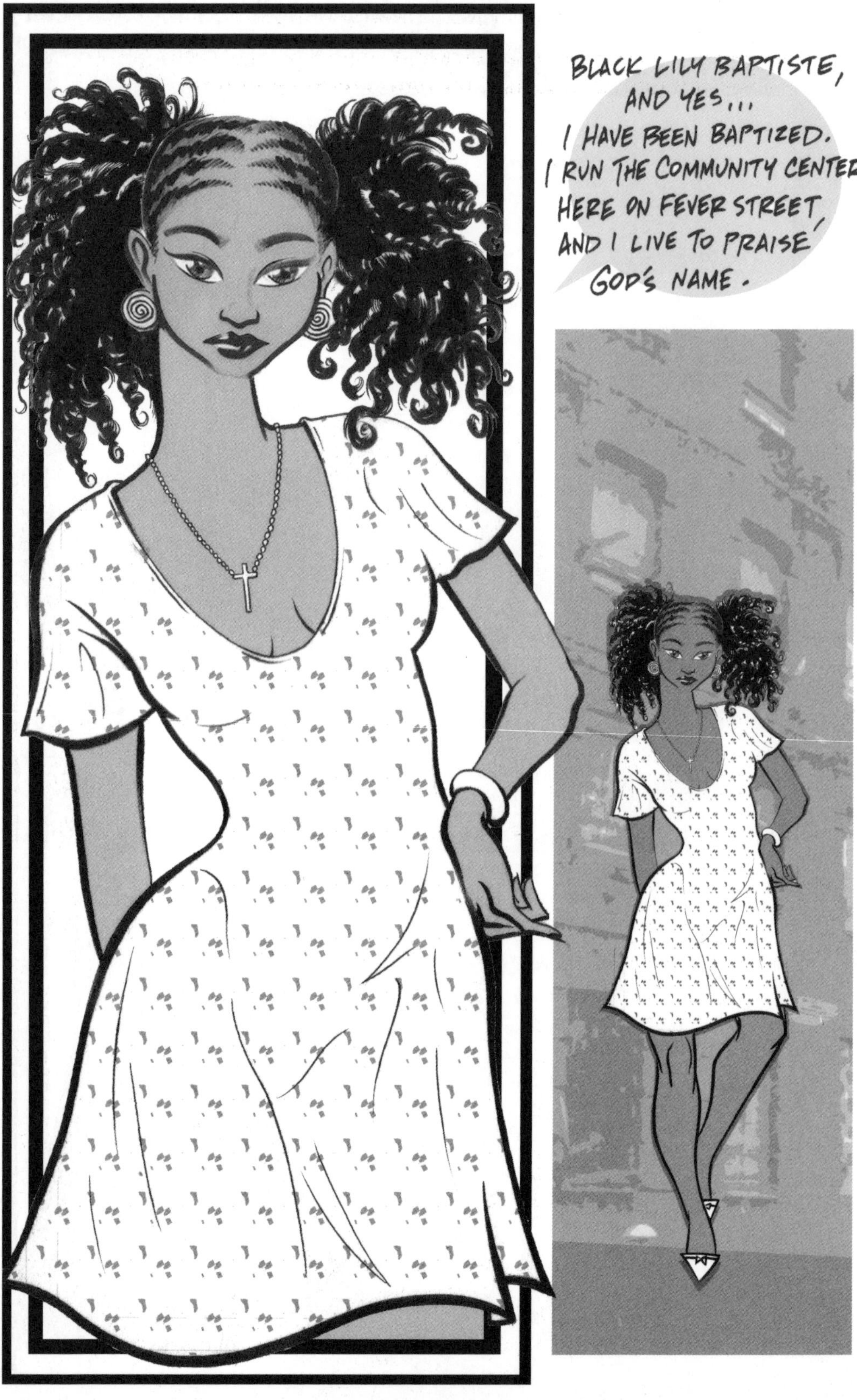
BLACK LILY BAPTISTE, AND YES... I HAVE BEEN BAPTIZED. I RUN THE COMMUNITY CENTER HERE ON FEVER STREET, AND I LIVE TO PRAISE GOD'S NAME.

invisible,
i drink deep
the air of summer,
a faint remembered
taste from
centuries past

so different from
that of my own
wretched underworld,
instead of
dried death
i savor the
aroma of life,
a fragrant
hint of hope
where i have
only known despair

invisible, i stand close
enough to taste
her breath,
the sweet cream in
her skin and hair,
the salty musk
of her pulsing blood

i bathe in the
blinding glare
of her firm,
unwavering faith

to be close to her
is to be close to Him

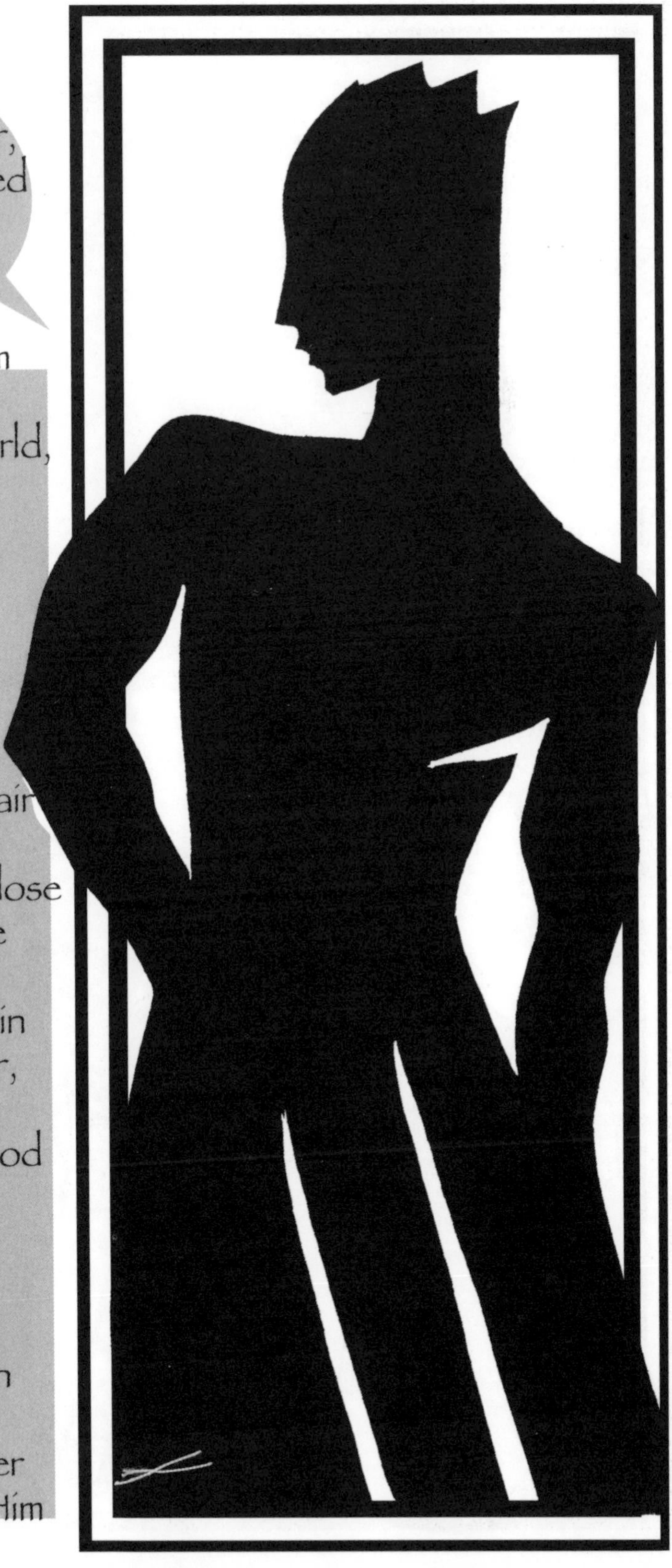

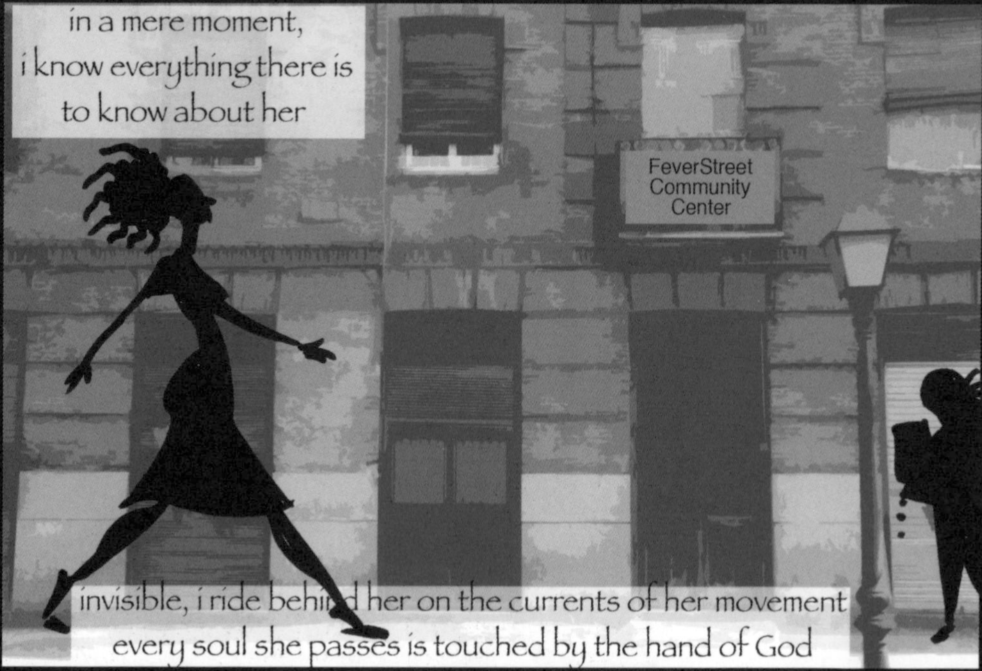
in a mere moment,
i know everything there is
to know about her
FeverStreet
Community
Center
invisible, i ride behind her on the currents of her movement
every soul she passes is touched by the hand of God

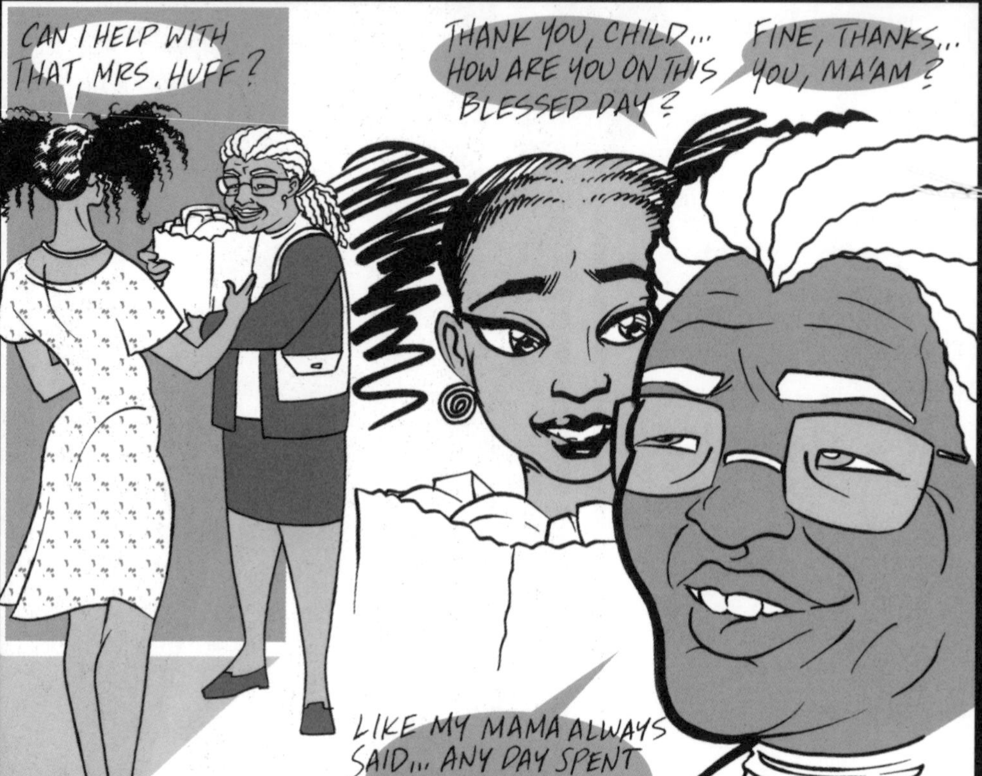
CAN I HELP WITH THAT, MRS. HUFF?
THANK YOU, CHILD... HOW ARE YOU ON THIS BLESSED DAY?
FINE, THANKS... YOU, MA'AM?
LIKE MY MAMA ALWAYS SAID... ANY DAY SPENT ABOVEGROUND IS BOUND TO BE A GOOD ONE.

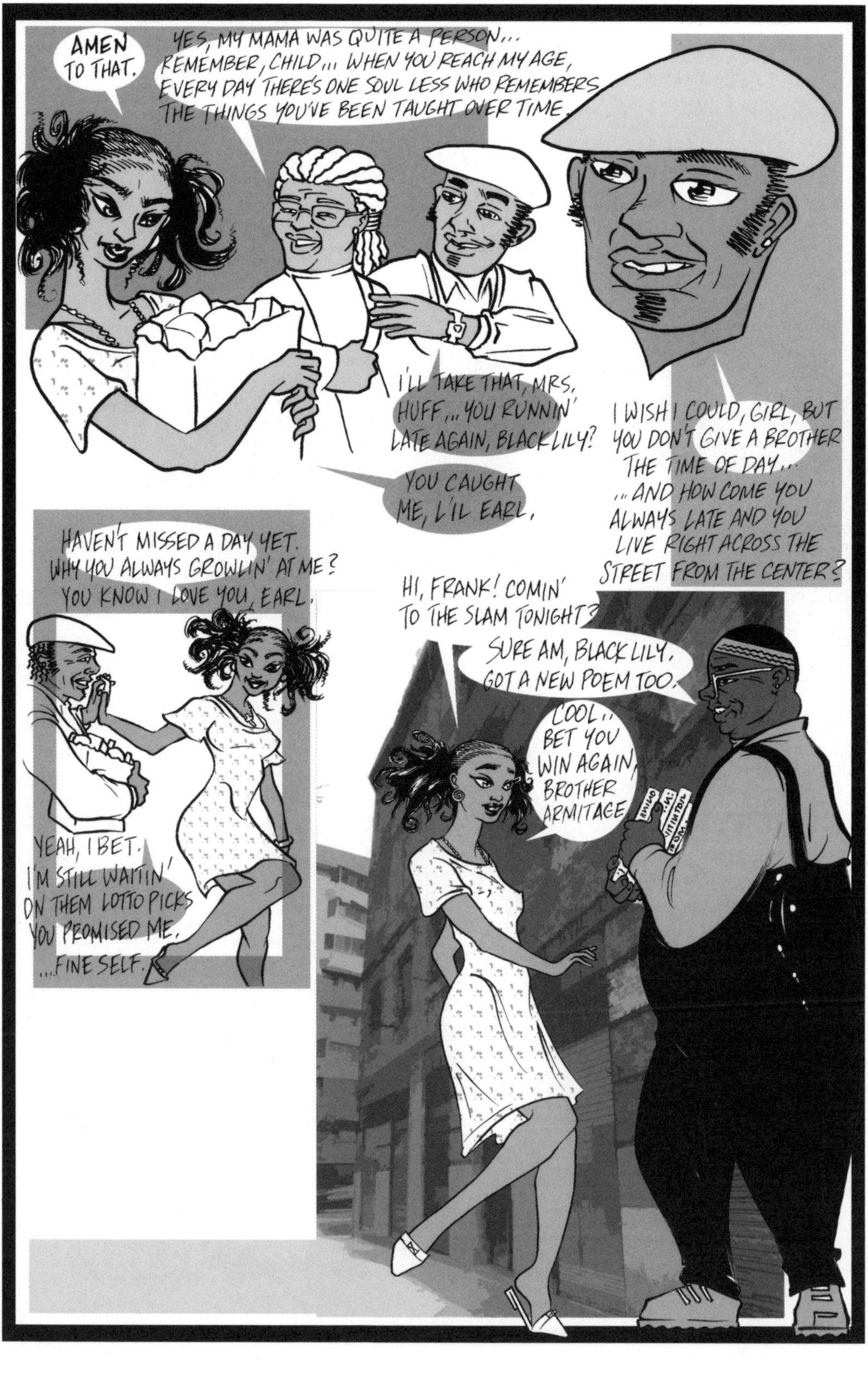

AMEN TO THAT.
YES, MY MAMA WAS QUITE A PERSON... REMEMBER, CHILD... WHEN YOU REACH MY AGE, EVERY DAY THERE'S ONE SOUL LESS WHO REMEMBERS THE THINGS YOU'VE BEEN TAUGHT OVER TIME.
I'LL TAKE THAT, MRS. HUFF... YOU RUNNIN' LATE AGAIN, BLACK LILY?
YOU CAUGHT ME, L'IL EARL.
I WISH I COULD, GIRL, BUT YOU DON'T GIVE A BROTHER THE TIME OF DAY...
...AND HOW COME YOU ALWAYS LATE AND YOU LIVE RIGHT ACROSS THE STREET FROM THE CENTER?
HAVEN'T MISSED A DAY YET. WHY YOU ALWAYS GROWLIN' AT ME? YOU KNOW I LOVE YOU, EARL.
YEAH, I BET. I'M STILL WAITIN' ON THEM LOTTO PICKS YOU PROMISED ME.
...FINE SELF.
HI, FRANK! COMIN' TO THE SLAM TONIGHT?
SURE AM, BLACK LILY. GOT A NEW POEM TOO.
COOL.. BET YOU WIN AGAIN, BROTHER ARMITAGE

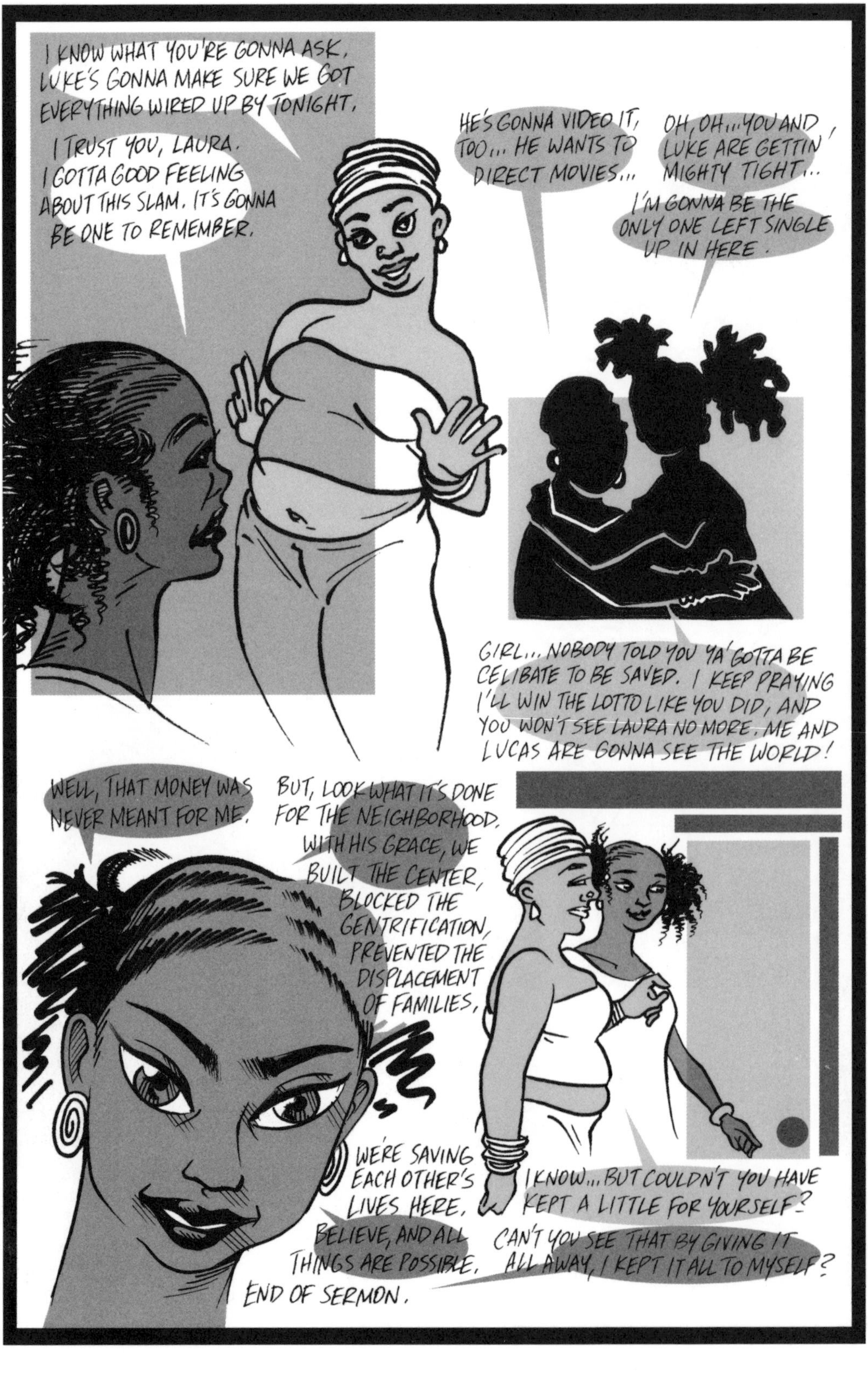
I KNOW WHAT YOU'RE GONNA ASK. LUKE'S GONNA MAKE SURE WE GOT EVERYTHING WIRED UP BY TONIGHT.
I TRUST YOU, LAURA. I GOTTA GOOD FEELING ABOUT THIS SLAM. IT'S GONNA BE ONE TO REMEMBER.
HE'S GONNA VIDEO IT, TOO... HE WANTS TO DIRECT MOVIES...
OH, OH... YOU AND LUKE ARE GETTIN' MIGHTY TIGHT...
I'M GONNA BE THE ONLY ONE LEFT SINGLE UP IN HERE.
GIRL... NOBODY TOLD YOU YA' GOTTA BE CELIBATE TO BE SAVED. I KEEP PRAYING I'LL WIN THE LOTTO LIKE YOU DID, AND YOU WON'T SEE LAURA NO MORE. ME AND LUCAS ARE GONNA SEE THE WORLD!
WELL, THAT MONEY WAS NEVER MEANT FOR ME.
BUT, LOOK WHAT IT'S DONE FOR THE NEIGHBORHOOD. WITH HIS GRACE, WE BUILT THE CENTER, BLOCKED THE GENTRIFICATION, PREVENTED THE DISPLACEMENT OF FAMILIES.
WE'RE SAVING EACH OTHER'S LIVES HERE. BELIEVE, AND ALL THINGS ARE POSSIBLE. END OF SERMON.
I KNOW... BUT COULDN'T YOU HAVE KEPT A LITTLE FOR YOURSELF?
CAN'T YOU SEE THAT BY GIVING IT ALL AWAY, I KEPT IT ALL TO MYSELF?

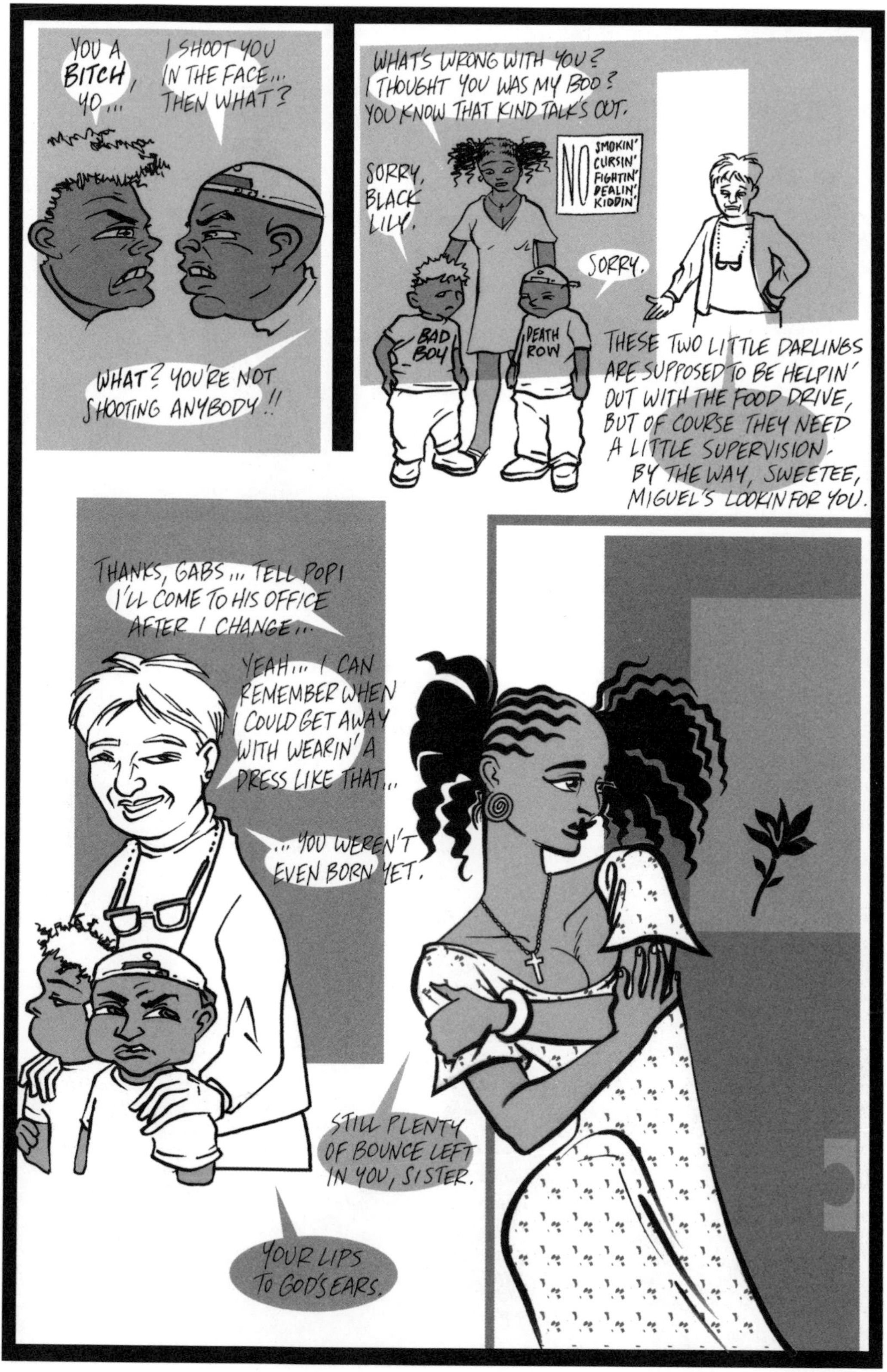
YOU A BITCH, YO...
I SHOOT YOU IN THE FACE... THEN WHAT?
WHAT? YOU'RE NOT SHOOTING ANYBODY!!
WHAT'S WRONG WITH YOU? I THOUGHT YOU WAS MY BOO? YOU KNOW THAT KIND TALK'S OUT.
NO SMOKIN' CURSIN' FIGHTIN' DEALIN' KIDDIN'
SORRY, BLACK LILY.
SORRY.
BAD BOY
DEATH ROW
THESE TWO LITTLE DARLINGS ARE SUPPOSED TO BE HELPIN' OUT WITH THE FOOD DRIVE, BUT OF COURSE THEY NEED A LITTLE SUPERVISION.
BY THE WAY, SWEETEE, MIGUEL'S LOOKIN FOR YOU.
THANKS, GABS... TELL POPI I'LL COME TO HIS OFFICE AFTER I CHANGE...
YEAH... I CAN REMEMBER WHEN I COULD GET AWAY WITH WEARIN' A DRESS LIKE THAT...
...YOU WEREN'T EVEN BORN YET.
STILL PLENTY OF BOUNCE LEFT IN YOU, SISTER.
YOUR LIPS TO GOD'S EARS.

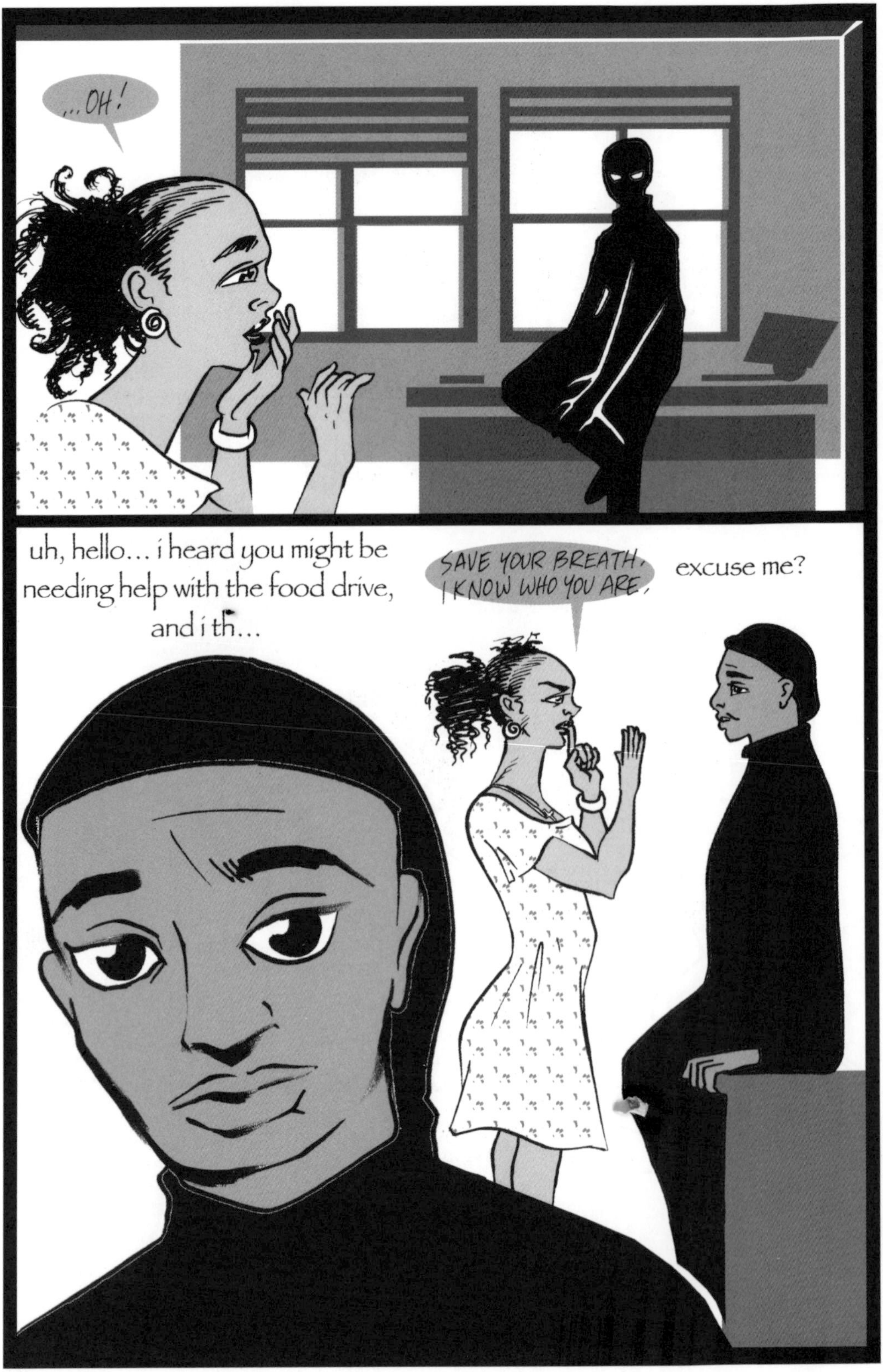
...OH!
uh, hello... i heard you might be needing help with the food drive, and i th...
SAVE YOUR BREATH, I KNOW WHO YOU ARE.
excuse me?

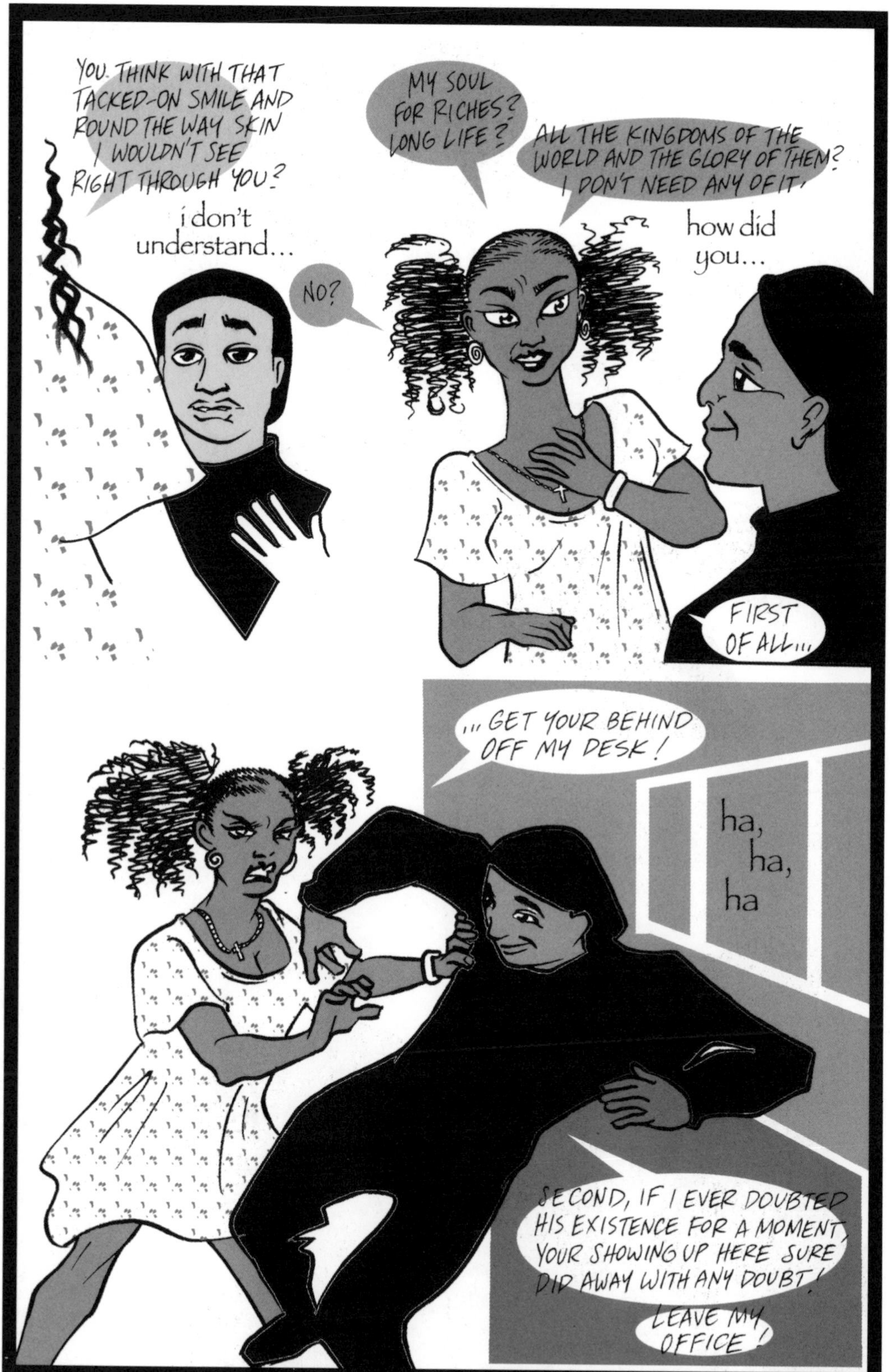
YOU THINK WITH THAT TACKED-ON SMILE AND ROUND THE WAY SKIN I WOULDN'T SEE RIGHT THROUGH YOU?
i don't understand...
NO?
MY SOUL FOR RICHES? LONG LIFE?
ALL THE KINGDOMS OF THE WORLD AND THE GLORY OF THEM? I DON'T NEED ANY OF IT.
how did you...
FIRST OF ALL...
...GET YOUR BEHIND OFF MY DESK!
ha, ha, ha
SECOND, IF I EVER DOUBTED HIS EXISTENCE FOR A MOMENT, YOUR SHOWING UP HERE SURE DID AWAY WITH ANY DOUBT!
LEAVE MY OFFICE!

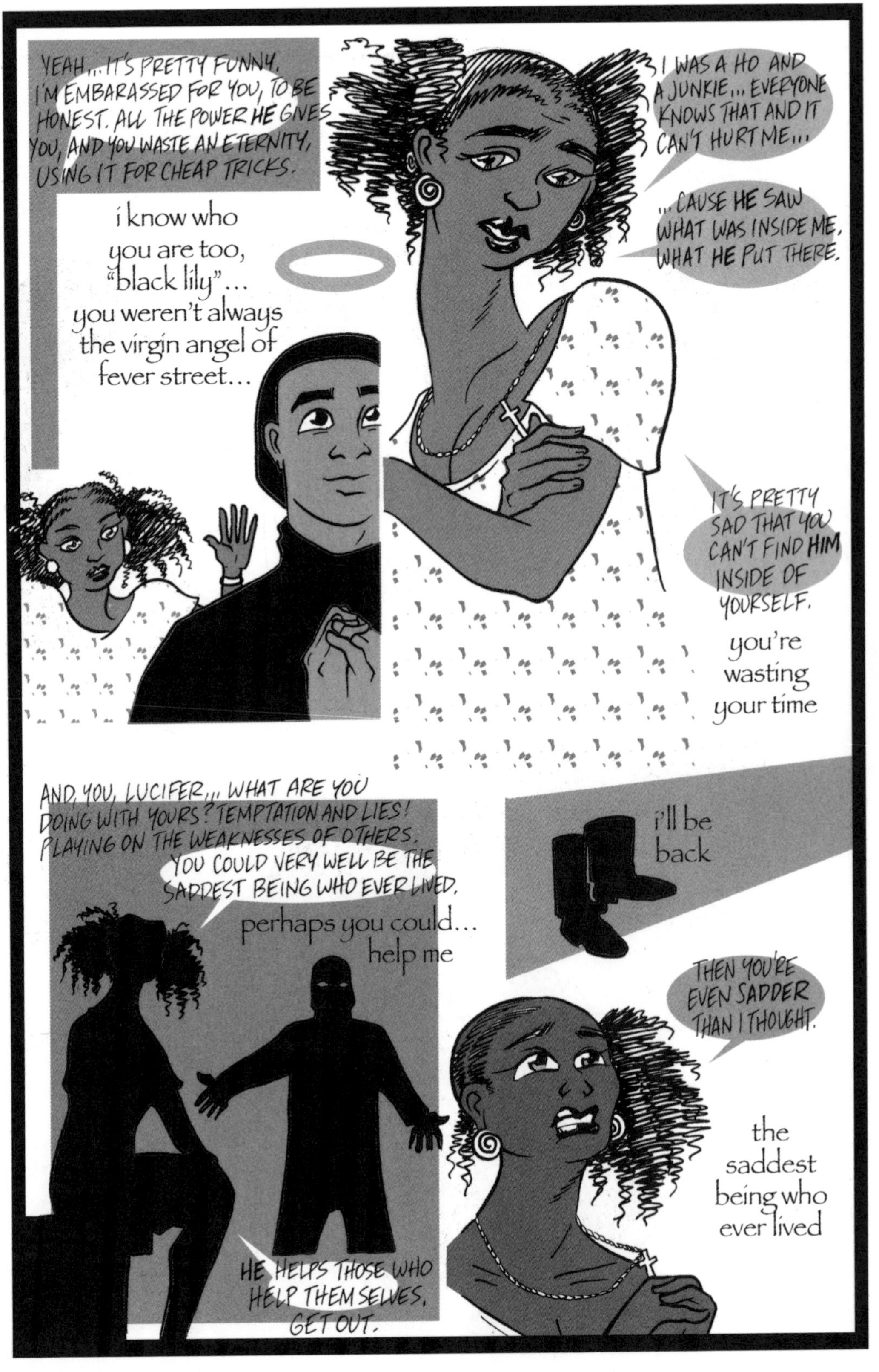
YEAH... IT'S PRETTY FUNNY. I'M EMBARASSED FOR YOU, TO BE HONEST. ALL THE POWER HE GIVES YOU, AND YOU WASTE AN ETERNITY, USING IT FOR CHEAP TRICKS.
i know who you are too, "black lily"... you weren't always the virgin angel of fever street...
I WAS A HO AND A JUNKIE... EVERYONE KNOWS THAT AND IT CAN'T HURT ME...
...CAUSE HE SAW WHAT WAS INSIDE ME, WHAT HE PUT THERE.
IT'S PRETTY SAD THAT YOU CAN'T FIND HIM INSIDE OF YOURSELF.
you're wasting your time
AND, YOU, LUCIFER... WHAT ARE YOU DOING WITH YOURS? TEMPTATION AND LIES! PLAYING ON THE WEAKNESSES OF OTHERS.
YOU COULD VERY WELL BE THE SADDEST BEING WHO EVER LIVED.
perhaps you could... help me
HE HELPS THOSE WHO HELP THEM SELVES. GET OUT.
i'll be back
THEN YOU'RE EVEN SADDER THAN I THOUGHT.
the saddest being who ever lived

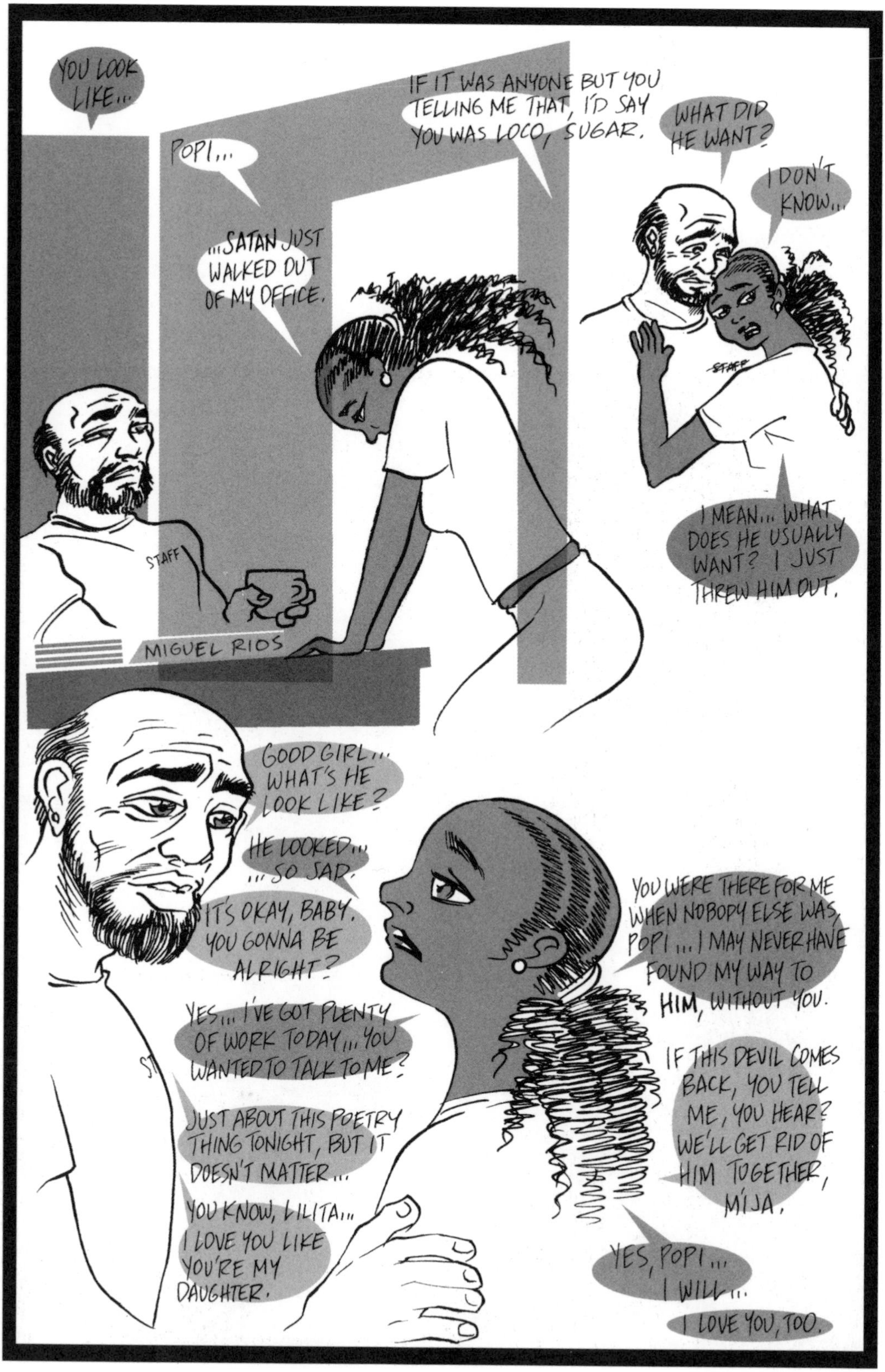
YOU LOOK LIKE...
POPI...
...SATAN JUST WALKED OUT OF MY OFFICE.
IF IT WAS ANYONE BUT YOU TELLING ME THAT, I'D SAY YOU WAS LOCO, SUGAR.
STAFF
MIGUEL RIOS
WHAT DID HE WANT?
I DON'T KNOW...
STAFF
I MEAN... WHAT DOES HE USUALLY WANT? I JUST THREW HIM OUT.
GOOD GIRL... WHAT'S HE LOOK LIKE?
HE LOOKED... ...SO SAD.
IT'S OKAY, BABY. YOU GONNA BE ALRIGHT?
YES... I'VE GOT PLENTY OF WORK TODAY... YOU WANTED TO TALK TO ME?
JUST ABOUT THIS POETRY THING TONIGHT, BUT IT DOESN'T MATTER...
YOU KNOW, LILITA... I LOVE YOU LIKE YOU'RE MY DAUGHTER.
YOU WERE THERE FOR ME WHEN NOBODY ELSE WAS, POPI... I MAY NEVER HAVE FOUND MY WAY TO HIM, WITHOUT YOU.
IF THIS DEVIL COMES BACK, YOU TELL ME, YOU HEAR? WE'LL GET RID OF HIM TOGETHER, MIJA.
YES, POPI... I WILL...
I LOVE YOU, TOO.

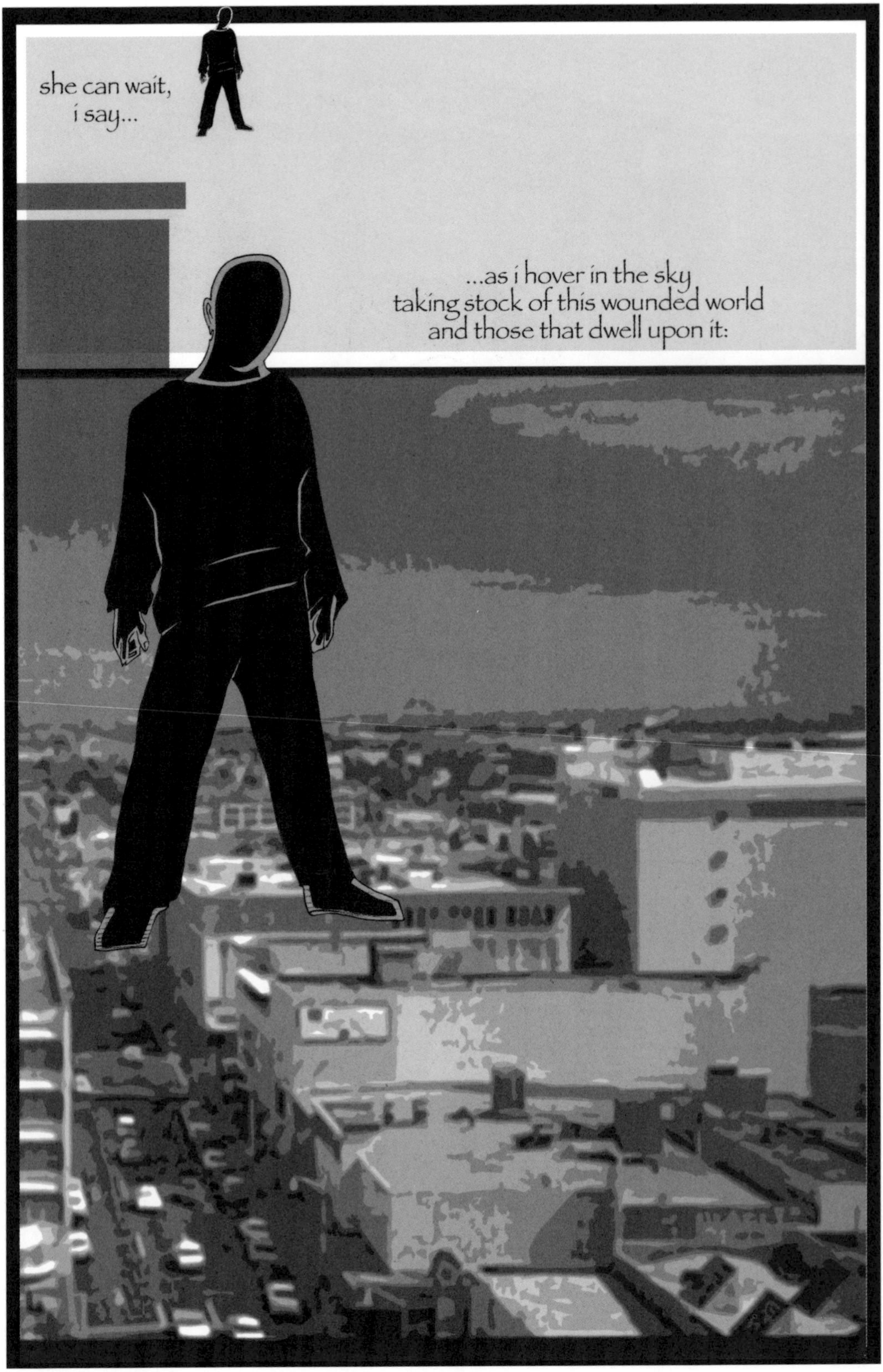
she can wait,
i say...
...as i hover in the sky
taking stock of this wounded world
and those that dwell upon it:

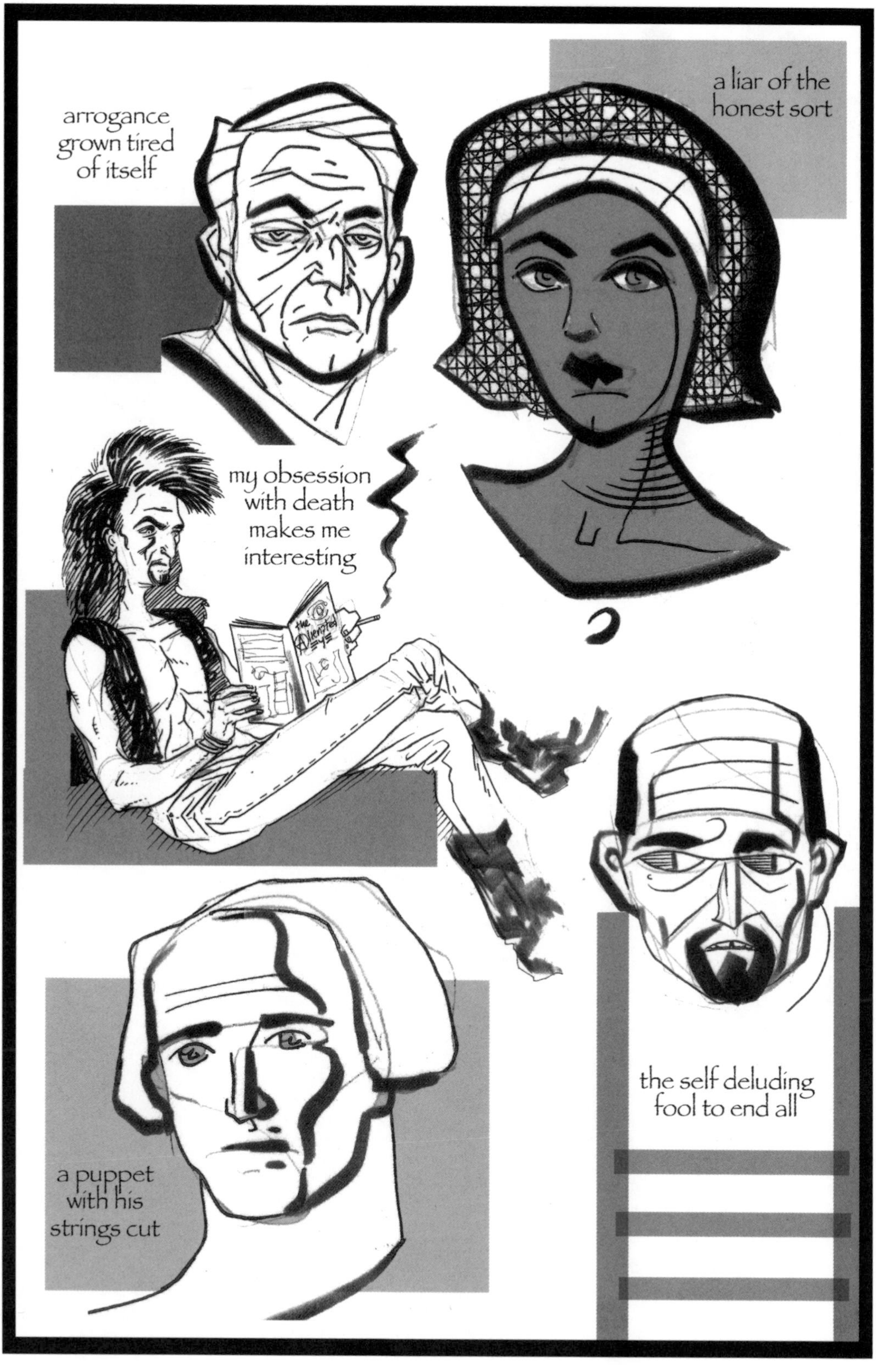
arrogance grown tired of itself
a liar of the honest sort
my obsession with death makes me interesting
the self deluding fool to end all
a puppet with his strings cut

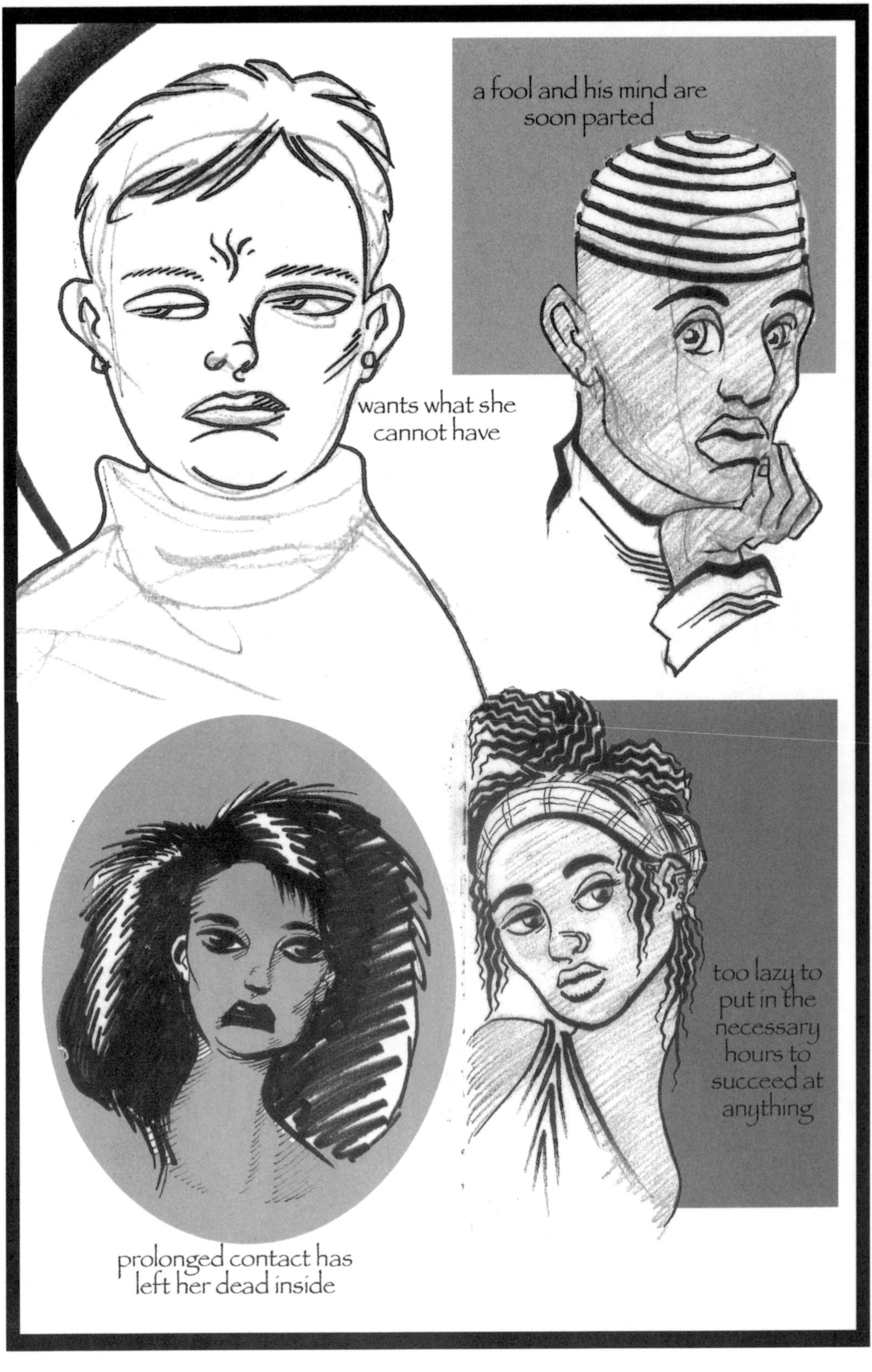
a fool and his mind are soon parted
wants what she cannot have
too lazy to put in the necessary hours to succeed at anything
prolonged contact has left her dead inside

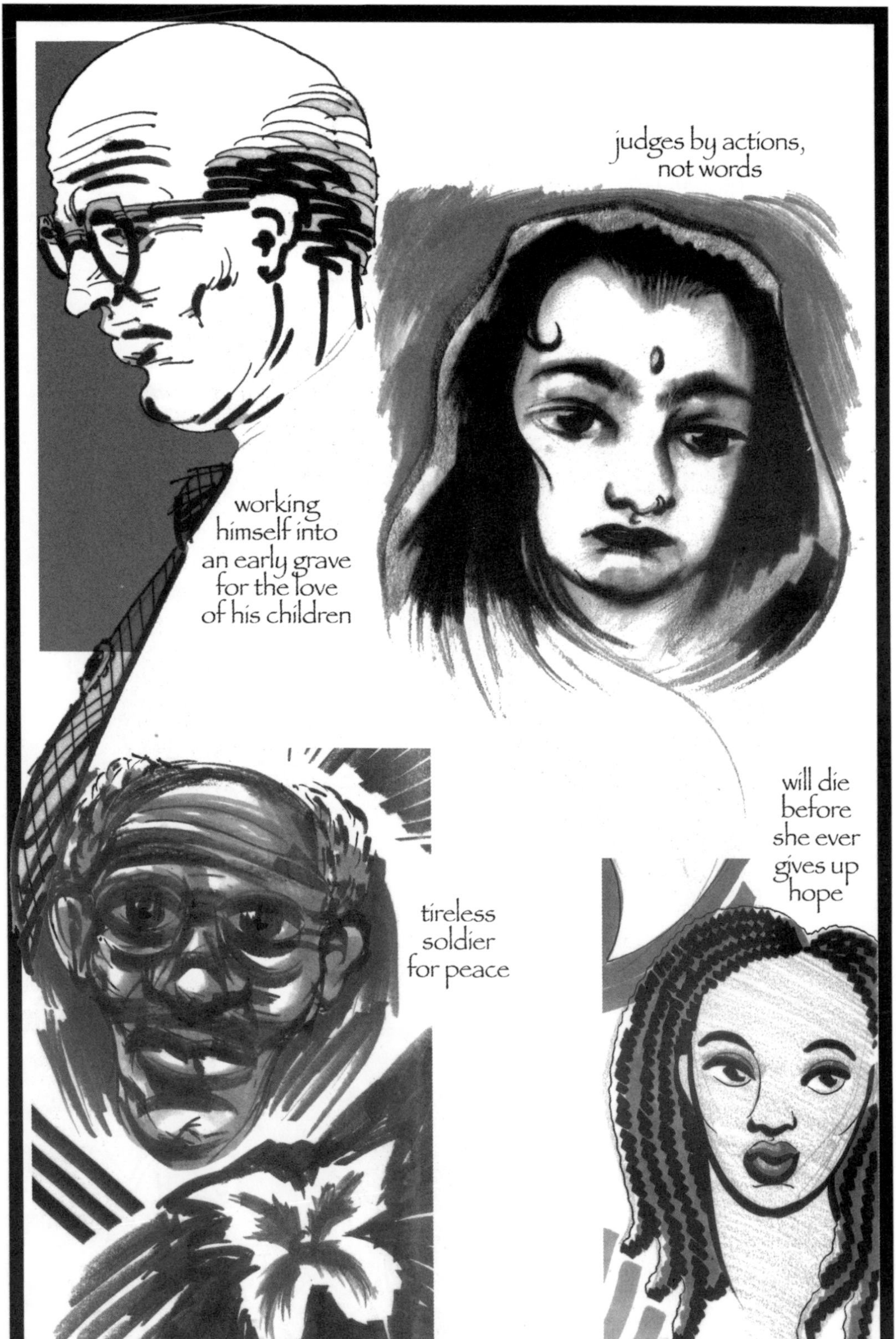
judges by actions, not words
working himself into an early grave for the love of his children
tireless soldier for peace
will die before she ever gives up hope

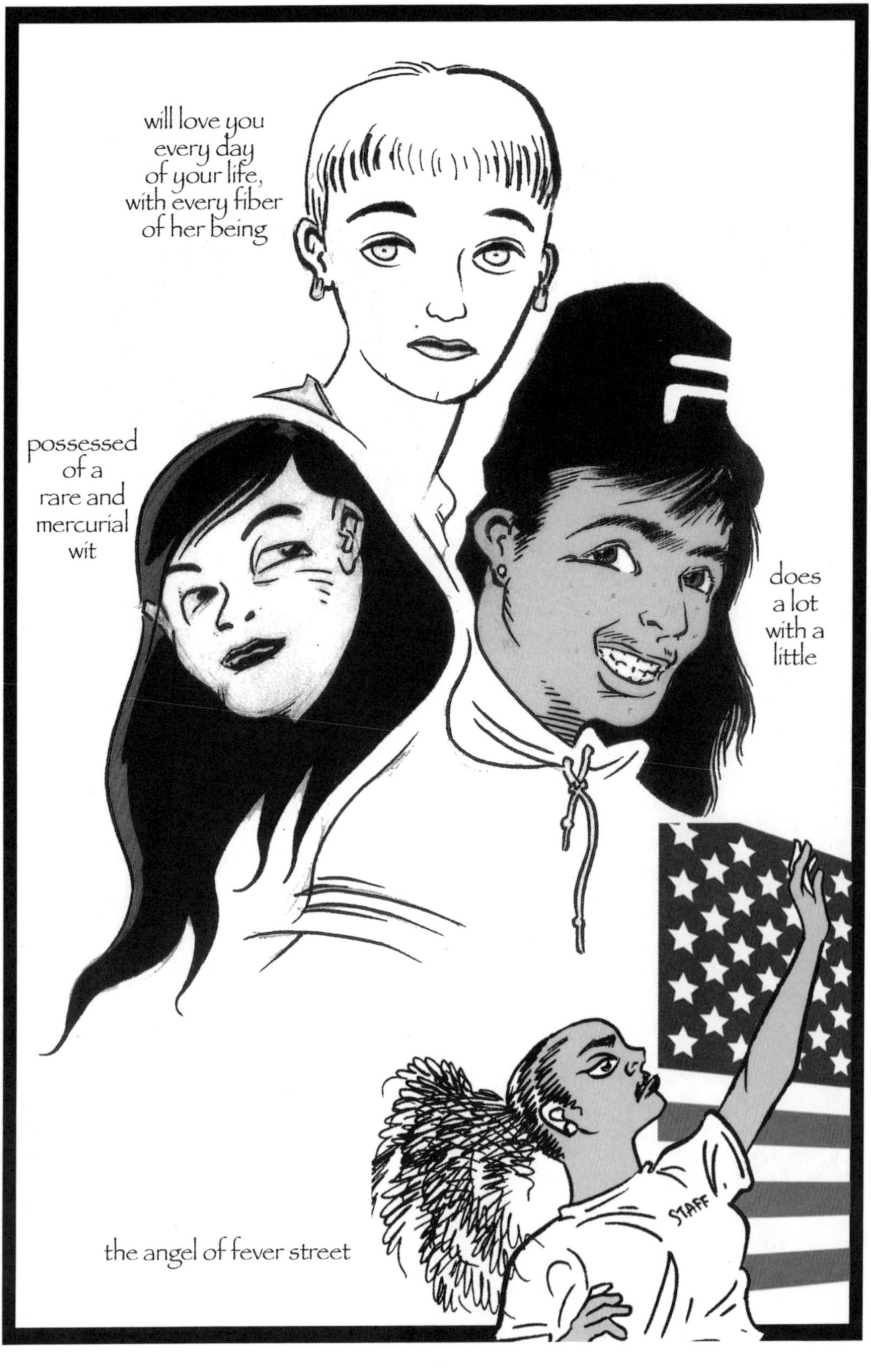
will love you
every day
of your life,
with every fiber
of her being
possessed
of a
rare and
mercurial
wit
does
a lot
with a
little
STAFF
the angel of fever street

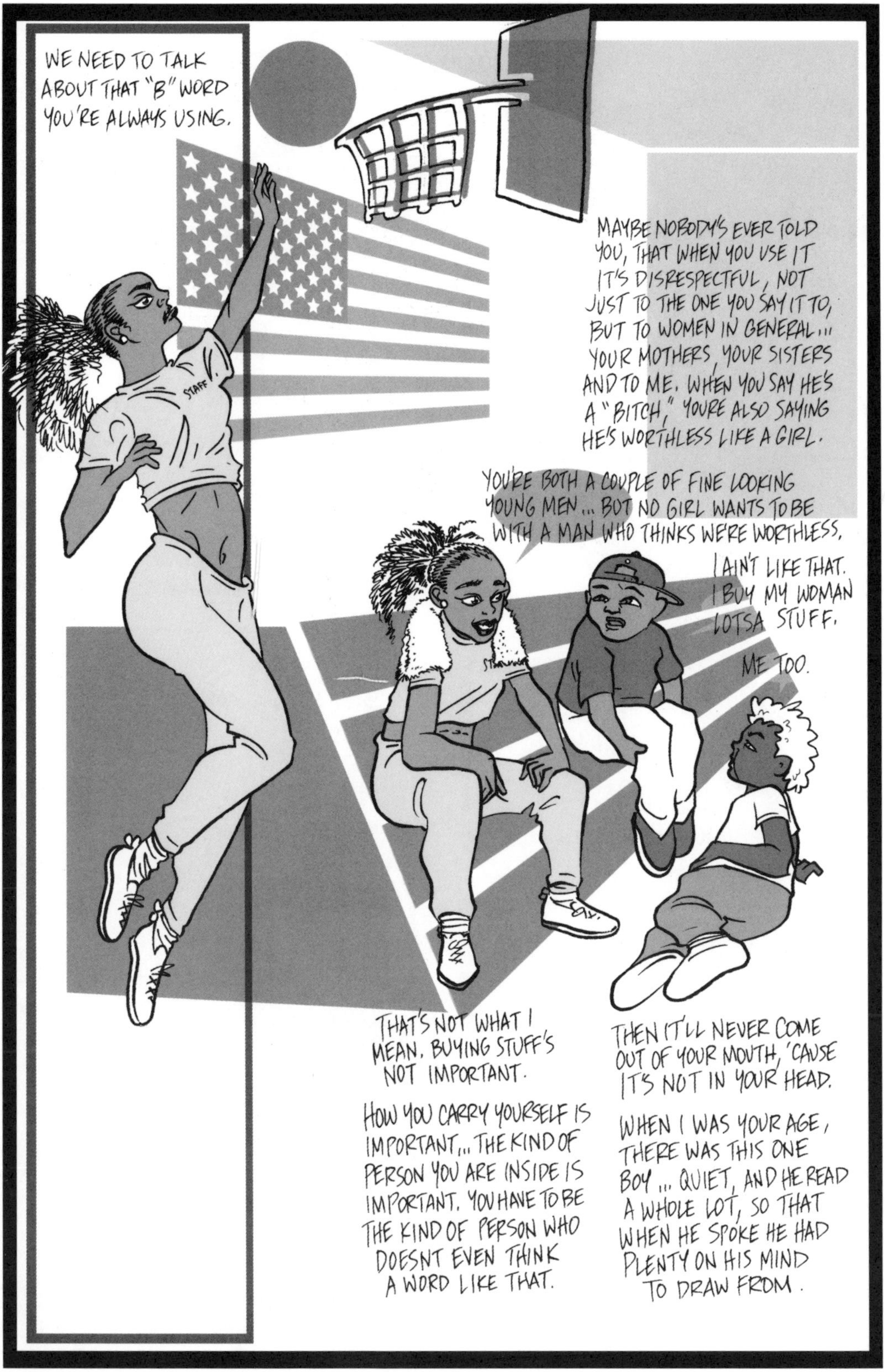
WE NEED TO TALK ABOUT THAT "B" WORD YOU'RE ALWAYS USING.
MAYBE NOBODY'S EVER TOLD YOU, THAT WHEN YOU USE IT IT'S DISRESPECTFUL, NOT JUST TO THE ONE YOU SAY IT TO, BUT TO WOMEN IN GENERAL... YOUR MOTHERS, YOUR SISTERS AND TO ME. WHEN YOU SAY HE'S A "BITCH," YOU'RE ALSO SAYING HE'S WORTHLESS LIKE A GIRL.
YOU'RE BOTH A COUPLE OF FINE LOOKING YOUNG MEN... BUT NO GIRL WANTS TO BE WITH A MAN WHO THINKS WE'RE WORTHLESS.
I AIN'T LIKE THAT. I BUY MY WOMAN LOTSA STUFF.
ME TOO.
STAFF
THAT'S NOT WHAT I MEAN. BUYING STUFF'S NOT IMPORTANT.
HOW YOU CARRY YOURSELF IS IMPORTANT... THE KIND OF PERSON YOU ARE INSIDE IS IMPORTANT. YOU HAVE TO BE THE KIND OF PERSON WHO DOESNT EVEN THINK A WORD LIKE THAT.
THEN IT'LL NEVER COME OUT OF YOUR MOUTH, 'CAUSE IT'S NOT IN YOUR HEAD.
WHEN I WAS YOUR AGE, THERE WAS THIS ONE BOY... QUIET, AND HE READ A WHOLE LOT, SO THAT WHEN HE SPOKE HE HAD PLENTY ON HIS MIND TO DRAW FROM.

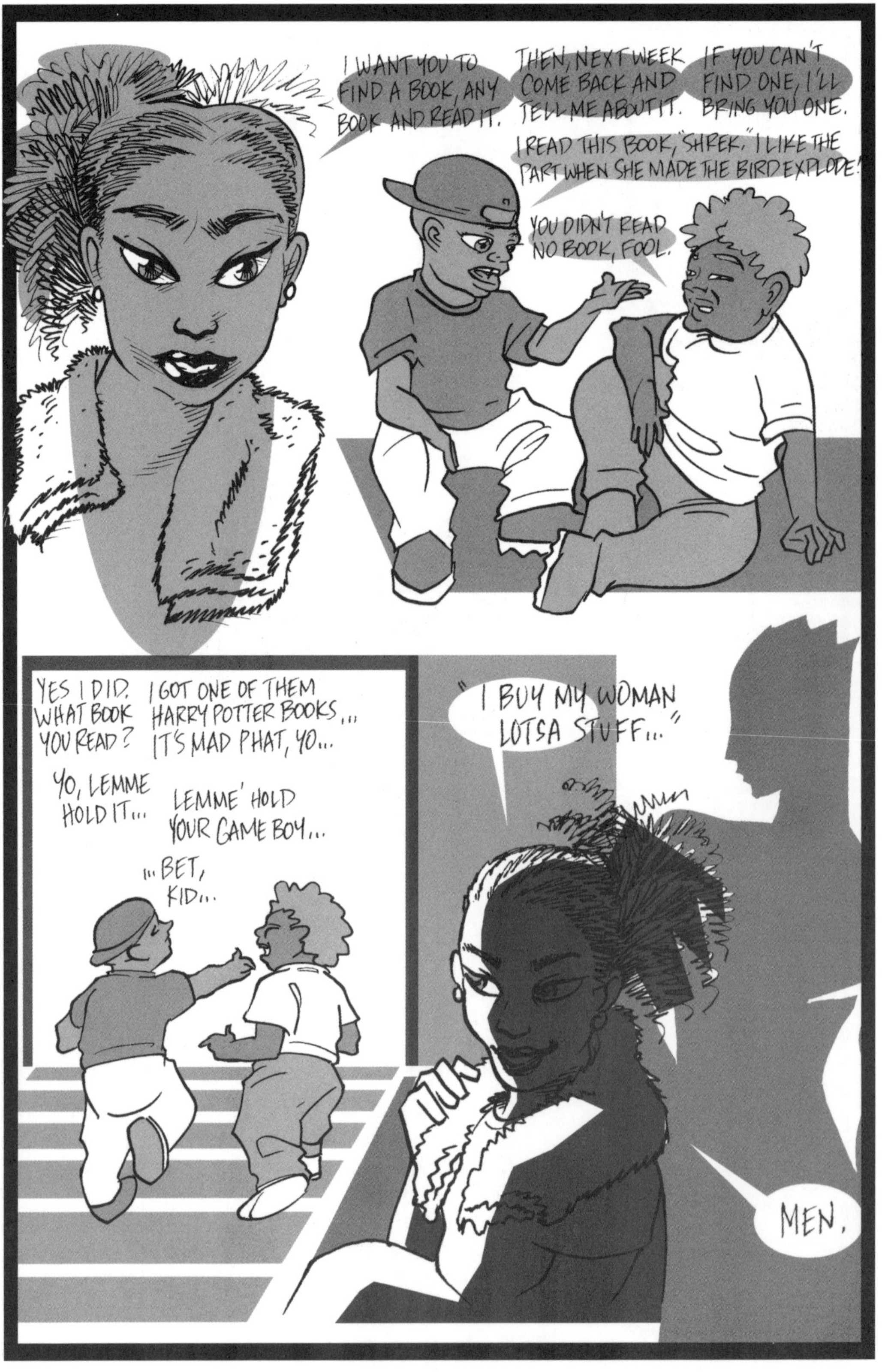
I WANT YOU TO FIND A BOOK, ANY BOOK AND READ IT.
THEN, NEXT WEEK COME BACK AND TELL ME ABOUT IT.
IF YOU CAN'T FIND ONE, I'LL BRING YOU ONE.
I READ THIS BOOK, "SHREK." I LIKE THE PART WHEN SHE MADE THE BIRD EXPLODE!
YOU DIDN'T READ NO BOOK, FOOL.
YES I DID. WHAT BOOK YOU READ?
I GOT ONE OF THEM HARRY POTTER BOOKS... IT'S MAD PHAT, YO...
YO, LEMME HOLD IT...
LEMME' HOLD YOUR GAME BOY...
...BET, KID...
"I BUY MY WOMAN LOTSA STUFF..."
MEN.

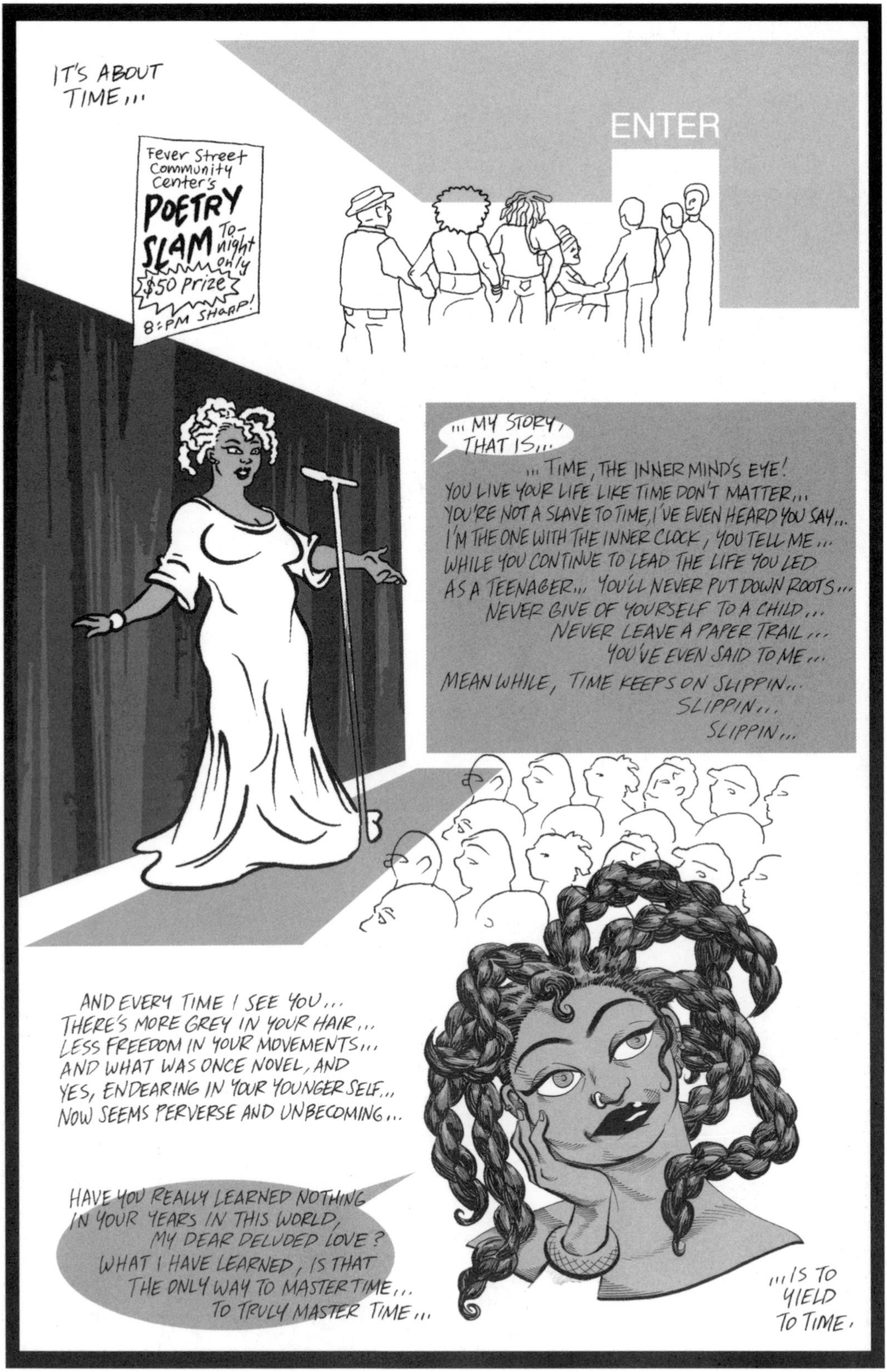
IT'S ABOUT TIME...
ENTER
Fever Street Community Center's POETRY SLAM To-night only $50 Prize 8:PM SHARP!
...MY STORY, THAT IS...
...TIME, THE INNER MIND'S EYE! YOU LIVE YOUR LIFE LIKE TIME DON'T MATTER... YOU'RE NOT A SLAVE TO TIME, I'VE EVEN HEARD YOU SAY... I'M THE ONE WITH THE INNER CLOCK, YOU TELL ME... WHILE YOU CONTINUE TO LEAD THE LIFE YOU LED AS A TEENAGER... YOU'LL NEVER PUT DOWN ROOTS... NEVER GIVE OF YOURSELF TO A CHILD... NEVER LEAVE A PAPER TRAIL... YOU'VE EVEN SAID TO ME... MEAN WHILE, TIME KEEPS ON SLIPPIN... SLIPPIN... SLIPPIN...
AND EVERY TIME I SEE YOU... THERE'S MORE GREY IN YOUR HAIR... LESS FREEDOM IN YOUR MOVEMENTS... AND WHAT WAS ONCE NOVEL, AND YES, ENDEARING IN YOUR YOUNGER SELF... NOW SEEMS PERVERSE AND UNBECOMING...
HAVE YOU REALLY LEARNED NOTHING IN YOUR YEARS IN THIS WORLD, MY DEAR DELUDED LOVE? WHAT I HAVE LEARNED, IS THAT THE ONLY WAY TO MASTER TIME... TO TRULY MASTER TIME...
...IS TO YIELD TO TIME.

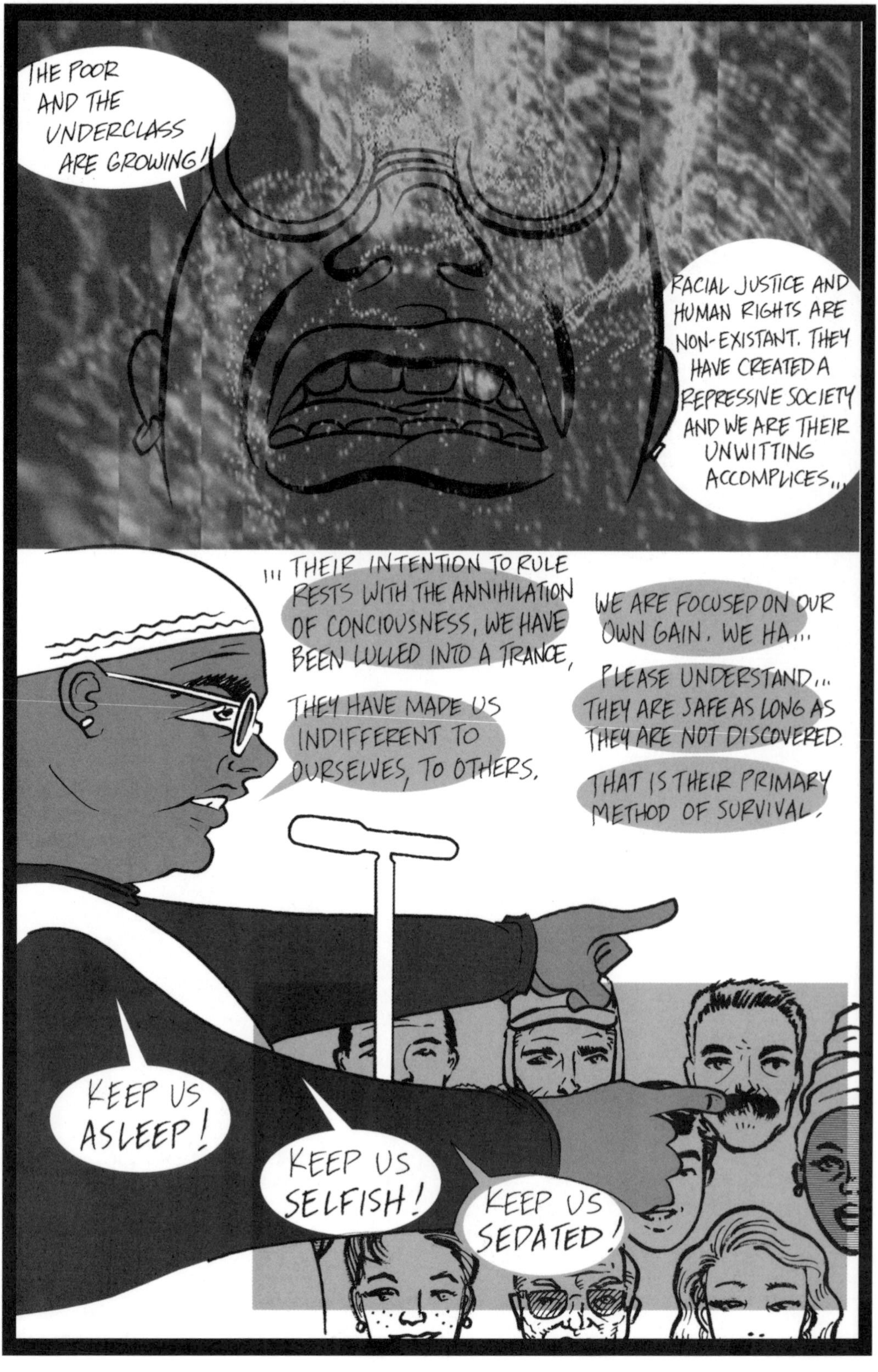
THE POOR AND THE UNDERCLASS ARE GROWING!
RACIAL JUSTICE AND HUMAN RIGHTS ARE NON-EXISTANT. THEY HAVE CREATED A REPRESSIVE SOCIETY AND WE ARE THEIR UNWITTING ACCOMPLICES...
...THEIR INTENTION TO RULE RESTS WITH THE ANNIHILATION OF CONCIOUSNESS, WE HAVE BEEN LULLED INTO A TRANCE,
THEY HAVE MADE US INDIFFERENT TO OURSELVES, TO OTHERS.
WE ARE FOCUSED ON OUR OWN GAIN. WE HA...
PLEASE UNDERSTAND... THEY ARE SAFE AS LONG AS THEY ARE NOT DISCOVERED.
THAT IS THEIR PRIMARY METHOD OF SURVIVAL.
KEEP US ASLEEP!
KEEP US SELFISH!
KEEP US SEDATED!

THEY ARE DISMANTLING THE SLEEPING MIDDLE CLASS.
MORE AND MORE PEOPLE ARE BECOMING POOR.
WE ARE THEIR CATTLE!
WE ARE BEING BRED FOR SLAVERY.
THE REVOLU...
I DREAMED THIS SPAGHETTI WESTERN LAST NIGHT... "A BULLET FOR EVERY BUSH," IT WAS CALLED, STARRING CLINT EASTWOOD! UHHH... NOT THE REAL ONE... HE'S DOWN WITH THE NEW WORLD ORDER POSSE.
NO, THIS WAS THE DREAM EASTWOOD, THE HEROIC ONE I LOVED AS A KID...
IN THE MOVIE, THIS GANG OF HOODLUMS TOOK OVER THE TOWN ROBBED AND ENSLAVED THE TOWNSPEOPLE AND RAPED THE BILL OF RIGHTS.
BUT ALONG COMES EASTWOOD- THE PALE RIDER!
HE CHASED THE VARMINTS OUTTA TOWN, OFF THE TIP OF FLORIDA AND INTO THE SEA...
I'M BLACK...
I'M PUERTO-RICAN...
I'M GAY...
...AND I AM FROM THE BRONX!
AM I BETTER THAN THE SUM OF MY PARTS?
PERHAPS...
...BUT MY PARTS ARE PRETTY DAMN GOOD, I'D SAY!

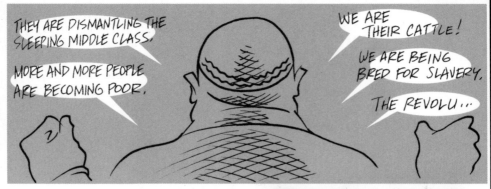

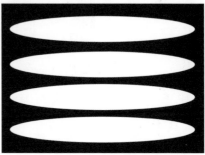

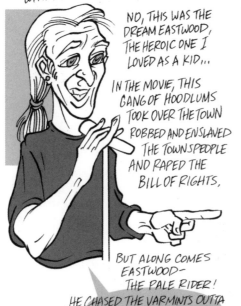

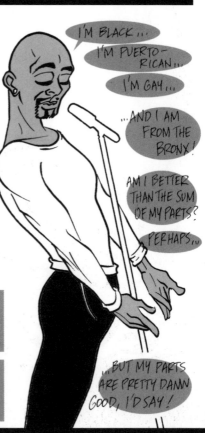

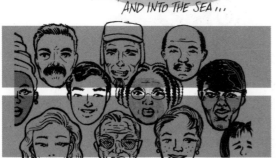

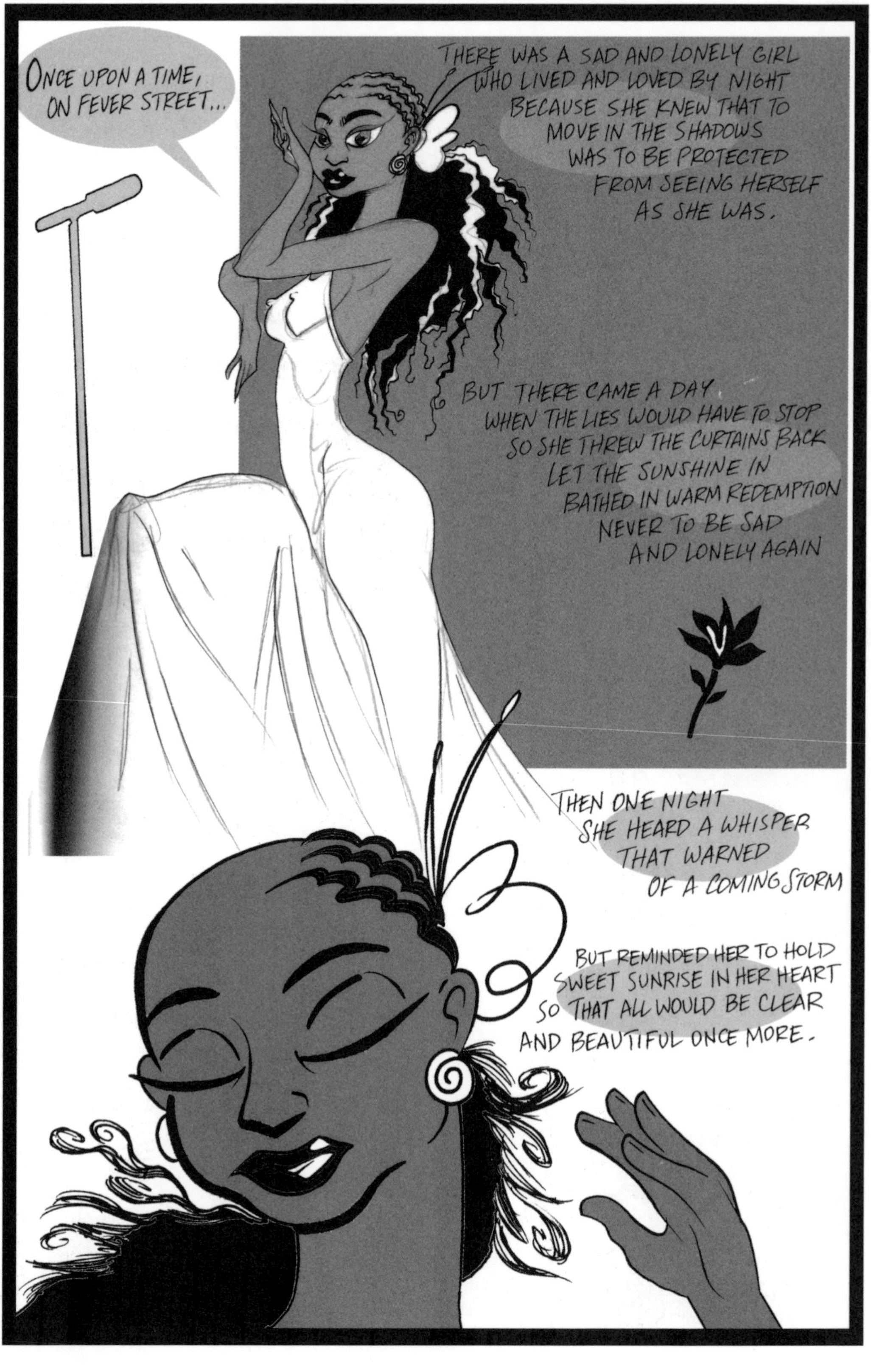

ONCE UPON A TIME, ON FEVER STREET...
THERE WAS A SAD AND LONELY GIRL WHO LIVED AND LOVED BY NIGHT BECAUSE SHE KNEW THAT TO MOVE IN THE SHADOWS WAS TO BE PROTECTED FROM SEEING HERSELF AS SHE WAS.
BUT THERE CAME A DAY WHEN THE LIES WOULD HAVE TO STOP SO SHE THREW THE CURTAINS BACK LET THE SUNSHINE IN BATHED IN WARM REDEMPTION NEVER TO BE SAD AND LONELY AGAIN
THEN ONE NIGHT SHE HEARD A WHISPER THAT WARNED OF A COMING STORM
BUT REMINDED HER TO HOLD SWEET SUNRISE IN HER HEART SO THAT ALL WOULD BE CLEAR AND BEAUTIFUL ONCE MORE.

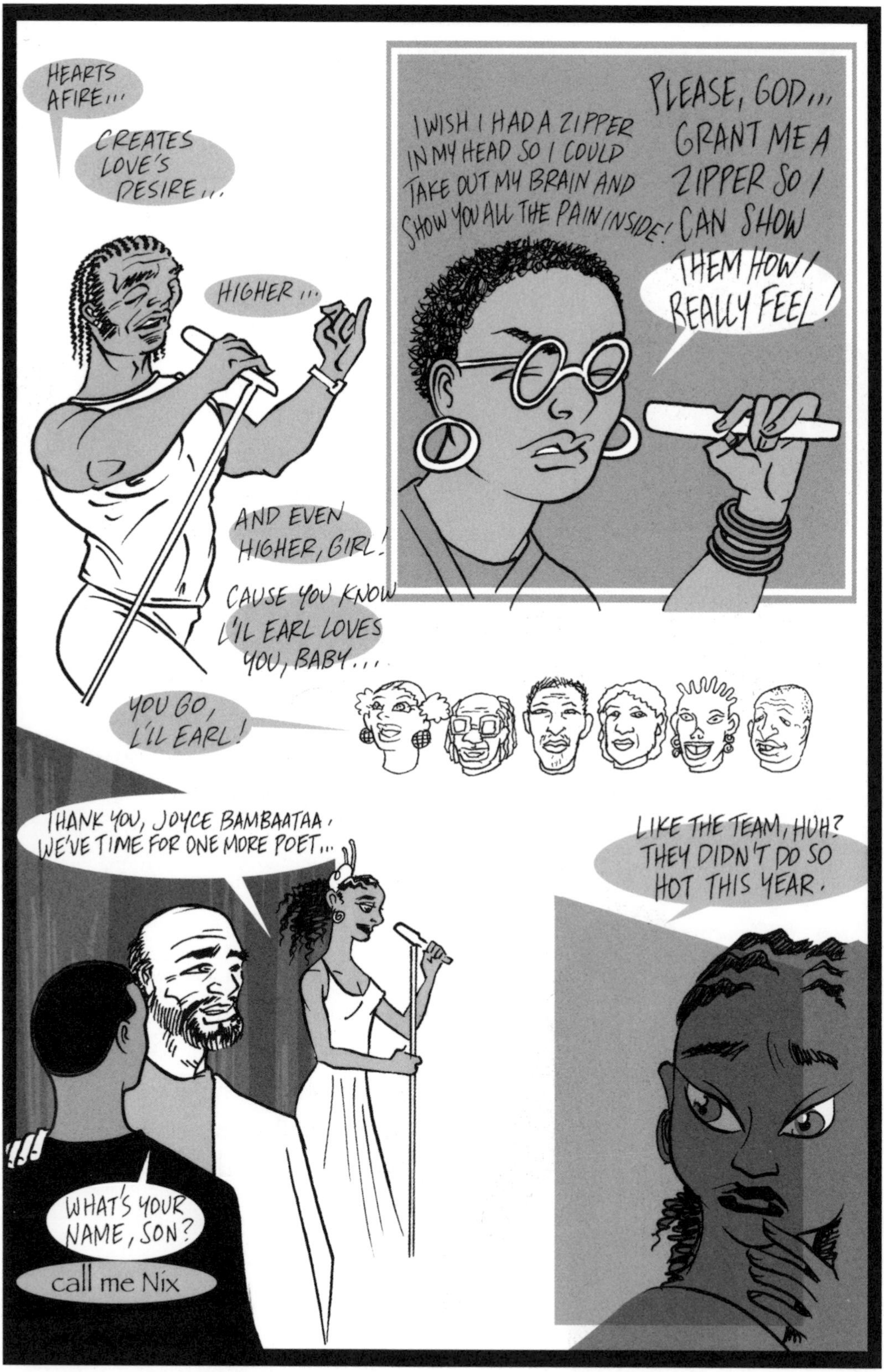
HEARTS AFIRE...
CREATES LOVE'S DESIRE...
HIGHER...
AND EVEN HIGHER, GIRL!
CAUSE YOU KNOW L'IL EARL LOVES YOU, BABY...
I WISH I HAD A ZIPPER IN MY HEAD SO I COULD TAKE OUT MY BRAIN AND SHOW YOU ALL THE PAIN INSIDE!
PLEASE, GOD... GRANT ME A ZIPPER SO I CAN SHOW
THEM HOW I REALLY FEEL!
YOU GO, L'IL EARL!
THANK YOU, JOYCE BAMBAATAA. WE'VE TIME FOR ONE MORE POET...
WHAT'S YOUR NAME, SON?
call me Nix
LIKE THE TEAM, HUH? THEY DIDN'T DO SO HOT THIS YEAR.

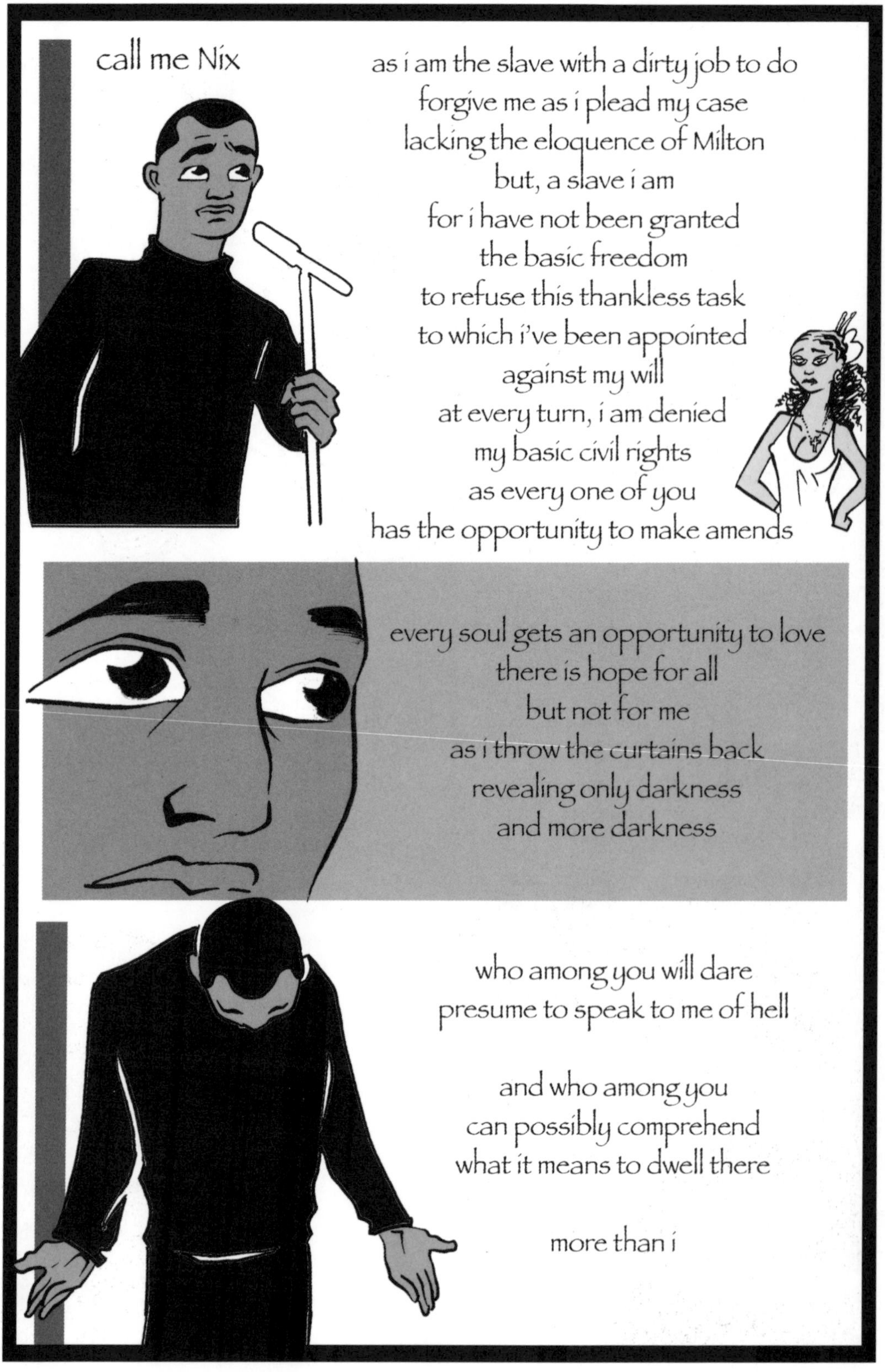

call me Nix

as i am the slave with a dirty job to do
forgive me as i plead my case
lacking the eloquence of Milton
but, a slave i am
for i have not been granted
the basic freedom
to refuse this thankless task
to which i've been appointed
against my will
at every turn, i am denied
my basic civil rights
as every one of you
has the opportunity to make amends

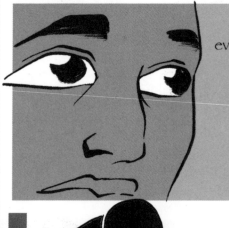

every soul gets an opportunity to love
there is hope for all
but not for me
as i throw the curtains back
revealing only darkness
and more darkness

who among you will dare
presume to speak to me of hell

and who among you
can possibly comprehend
what it means to dwell there

more than i

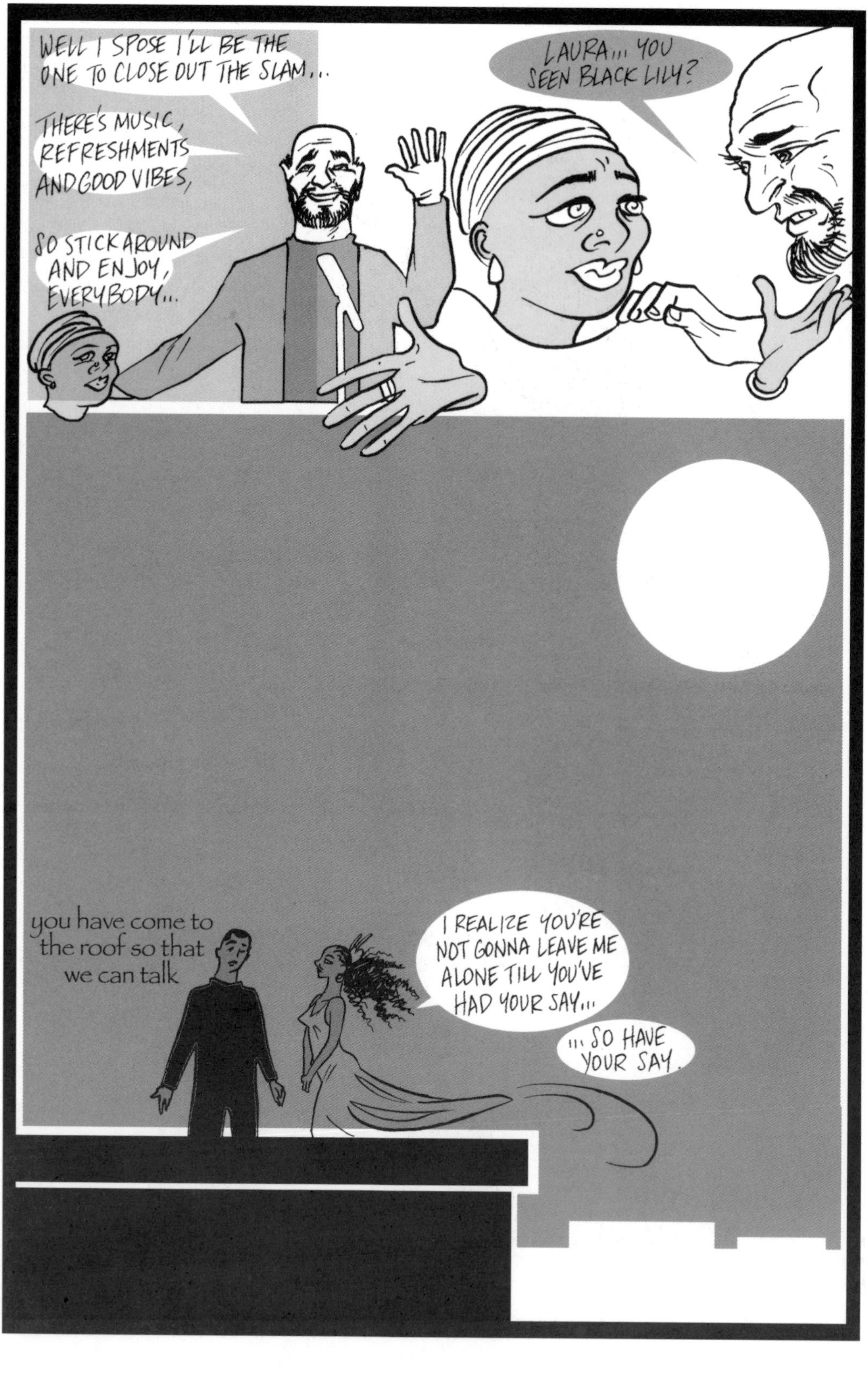
WELL I SPOSE I'LL BE THE ONE TO CLOSE OUT THE SLAM...
THERE'S MUSIC, REFRESHMENTS AND GOOD VIBES,
SO STICK AROUND AND ENJOY, EVERYBODY...
LAURA... YOU SEEN BLACK LILY?
you have come to the roof so that we can talk
I REALIZE YOU'RE NOT GONNA LEAVE ME ALONE TILL YOU'VE HAD YOUR SAY...
...SO HAVE YOUR SAY.

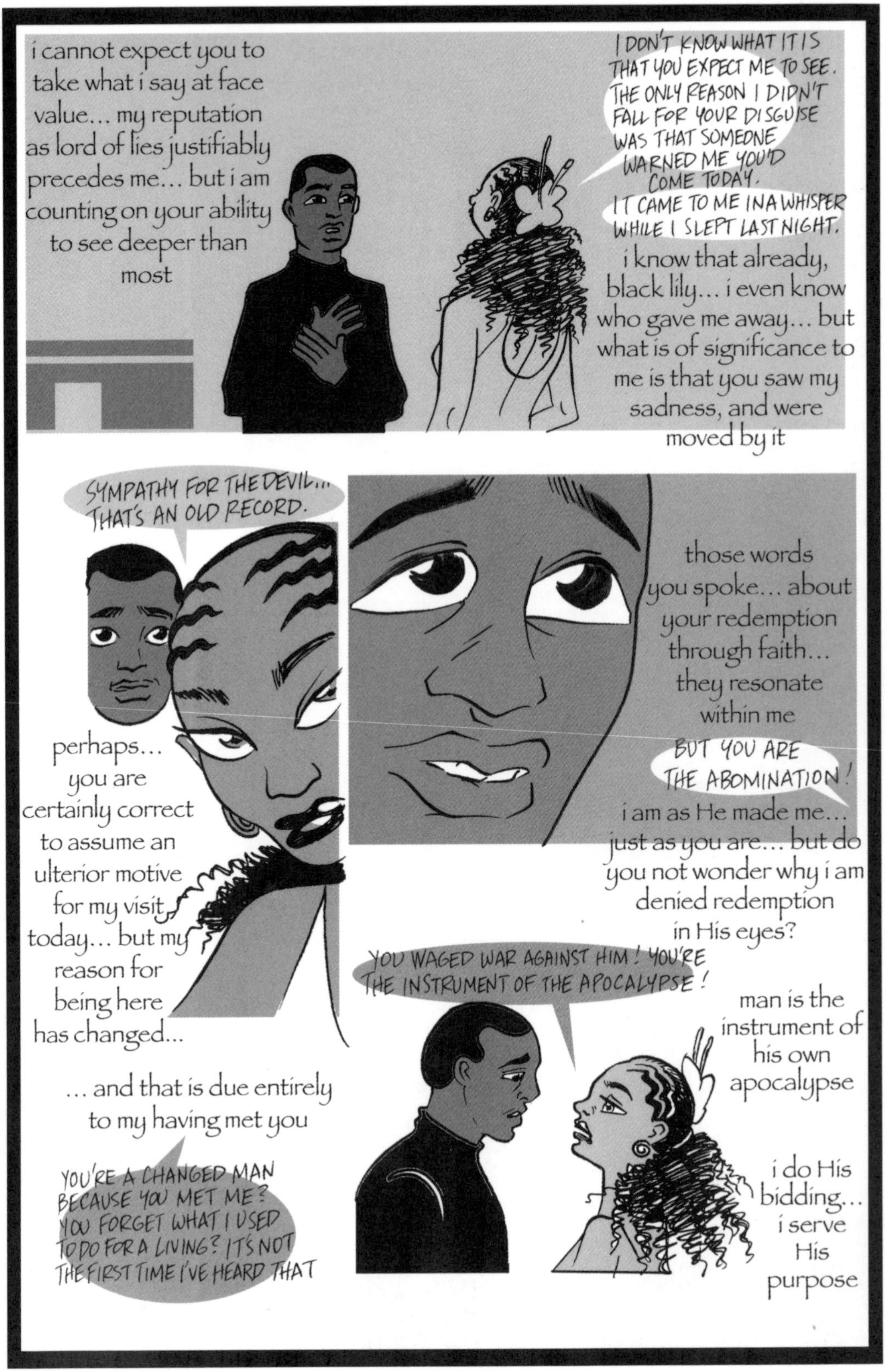

i cannot expect you to take what i say at face value... my reputation as lord of lies justifiably precedes me... but i am counting on your ability to see deeper than most
I DON'T KNOW WHAT IT IS THAT YOU EXPECT ME TO SEE. THE ONLY REASON I DIDN'T FALL FOR YOUR DISGUISE WAS THAT SOMEONE WARNED ME YOU'D COME TODAY.
IT CAME TO ME IN A WHISPER WHILE I SLEPT LAST NIGHT.
i know that already, black lily... i even know who gave me away... but what is of significance to me is that you saw my sadness, and were moved by it
SYMPATHY FOR THE DEVIL... THAT'S AN OLD RECORD.
perhaps... you are certainly correct to assume an ulterior motive for my visit today... but my reason for being here has changed...
... and that is due entirely to my having met you
YOU'RE A CHANGED MAN BECAUSE YOU MET ME? YOU FORGET WHAT I USED TO DO FOR A LIVING? IT'S NOT THE FIRST TIME I'VE HEARD THAT
those words you spoke... about your redemption through faith... they resonate within me
BUT YOU ARE THE ABOMINATION!
i am as He made me... just as you are... but do you not wonder why i am denied redemption in His eyes?
YOU WAGED WAR AGAINST HIM! YOU'RE THE INSTRUMENT OF THE APOCALYPSE!
man is the instrument of his own apocalypse
i do His bidding... i serve His purpose

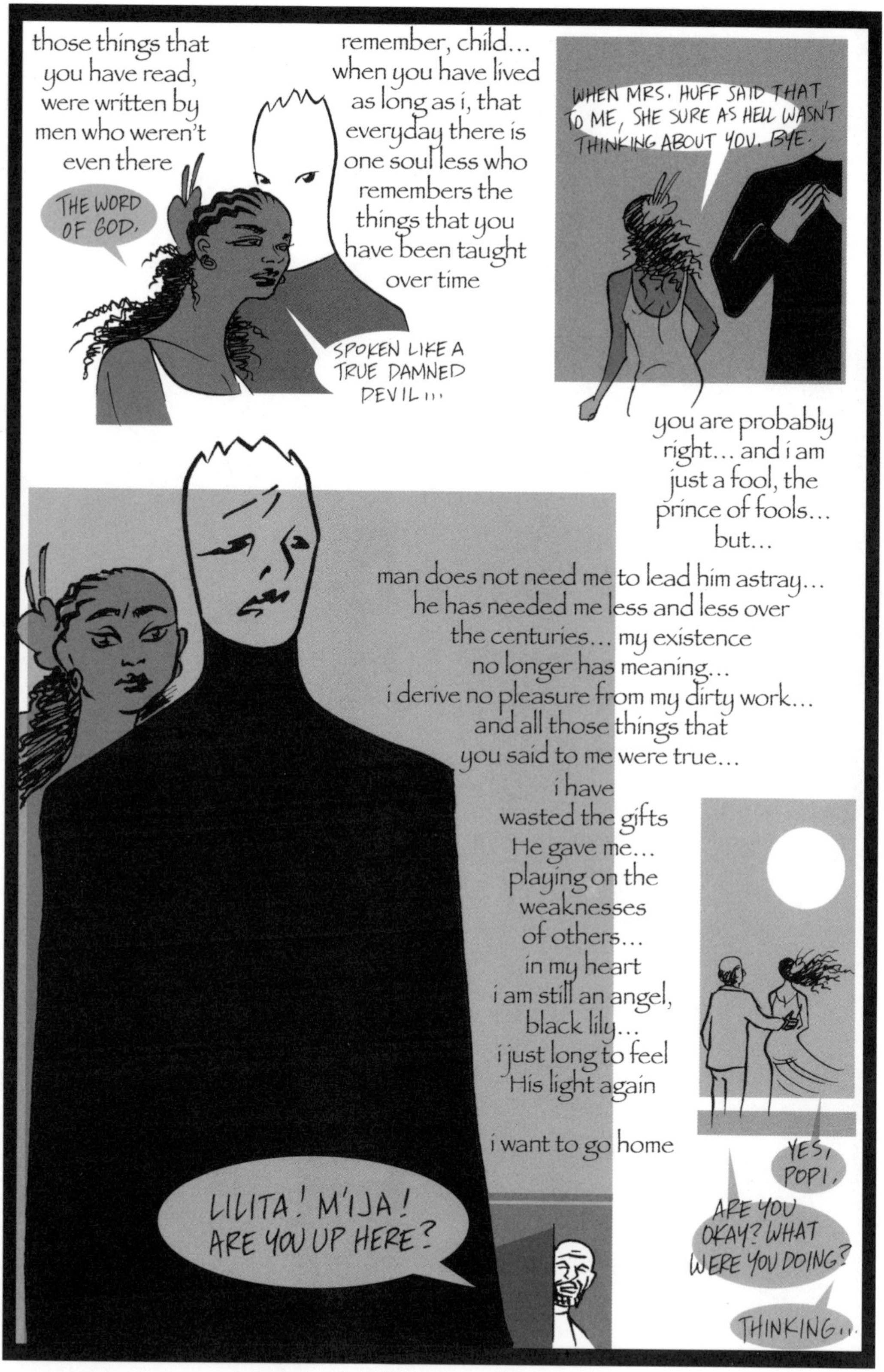

those things that you have read, were written by men who weren't even there
THE WORD OF GOD.
remember, child... when you have lived as long as i, that everyday there is one soul less who remembers the things that you have been taught over time
SPOKEN LIKE A TRUE DAMNED DEVIL...
WHEN MRS. HUFF SAID THAT TO ME, SHE SURE AS HELL WASN'T THINKING ABOUT YOU. BYE.
you are probably right... and i am just a fool, the prince of fools... but...
man does not need me to lead him astray... he has needed me less and less over the centuries... my existence no longer has meaning... i derive no pleasure from my dirty work... and all those things that you said to me were true...
i have wasted the gifts He gave me... playing on the weaknesses of others... in my heart i am still an angel, black lily... i just long to feel His light again
i want to go home
LILITA! M'IJA! ARE YOU UP HERE?
YES, POPI.
ARE YOU OKAY? WHAT WERE YOU DOING?
THINKING...

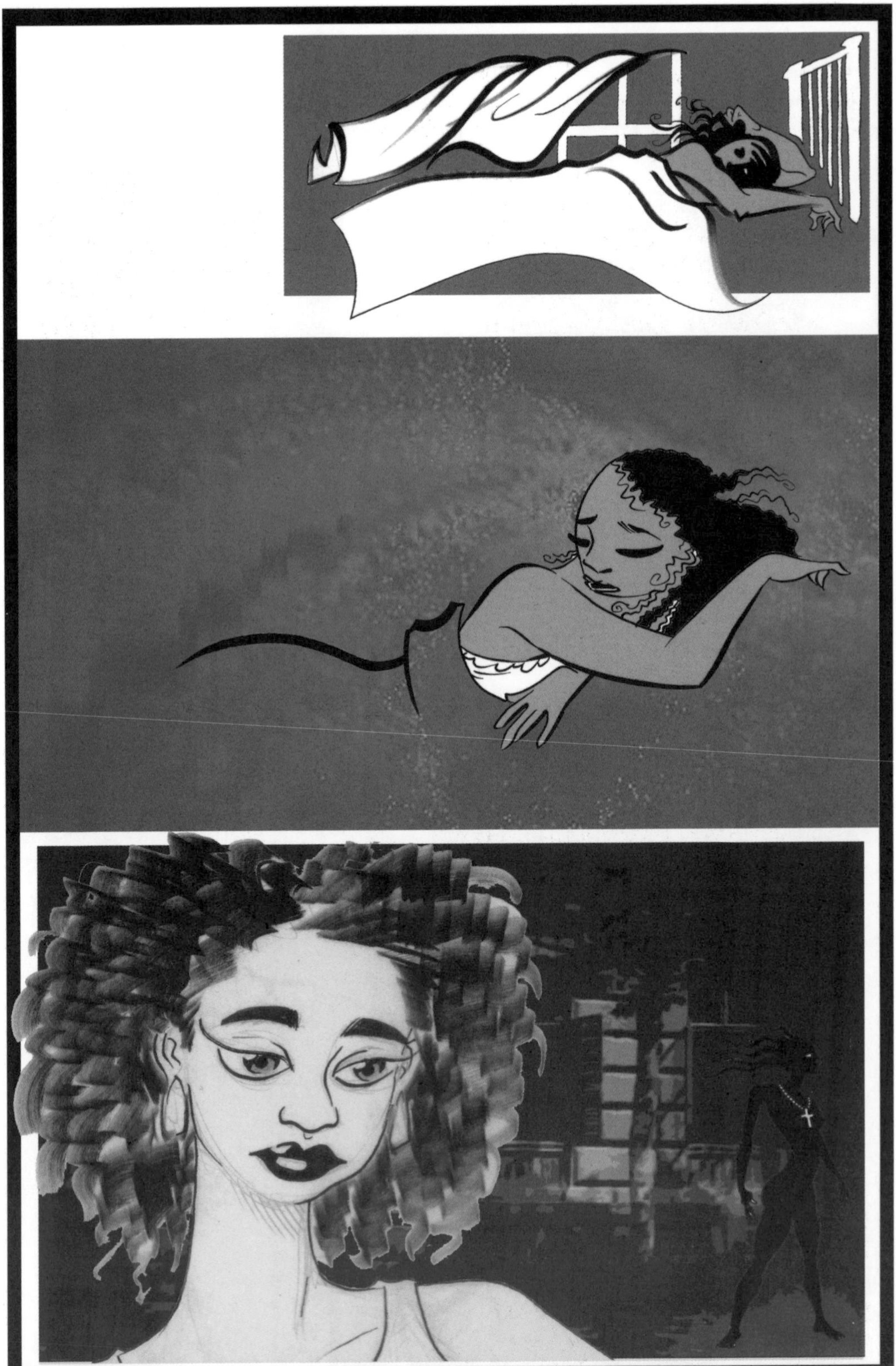

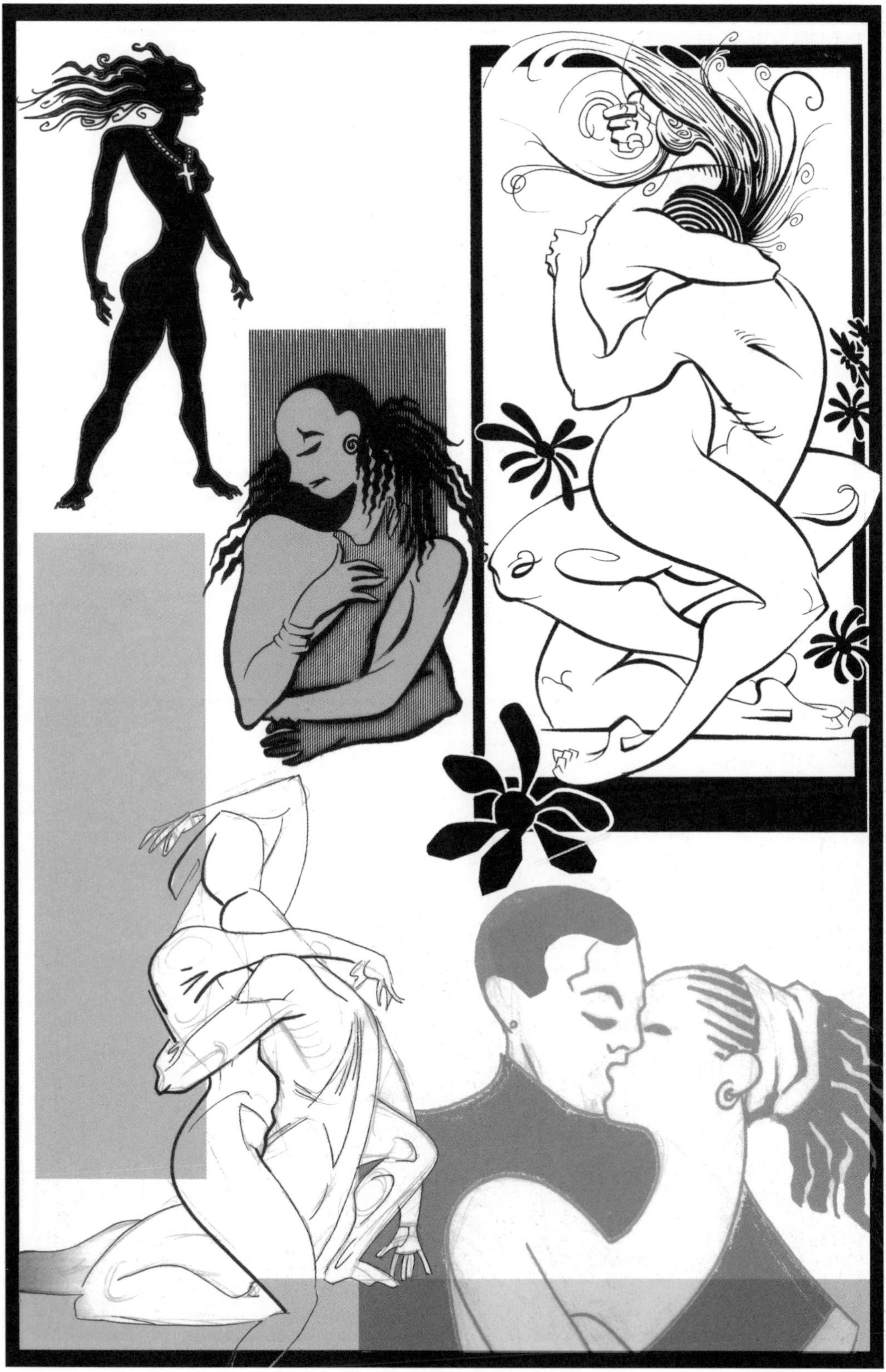

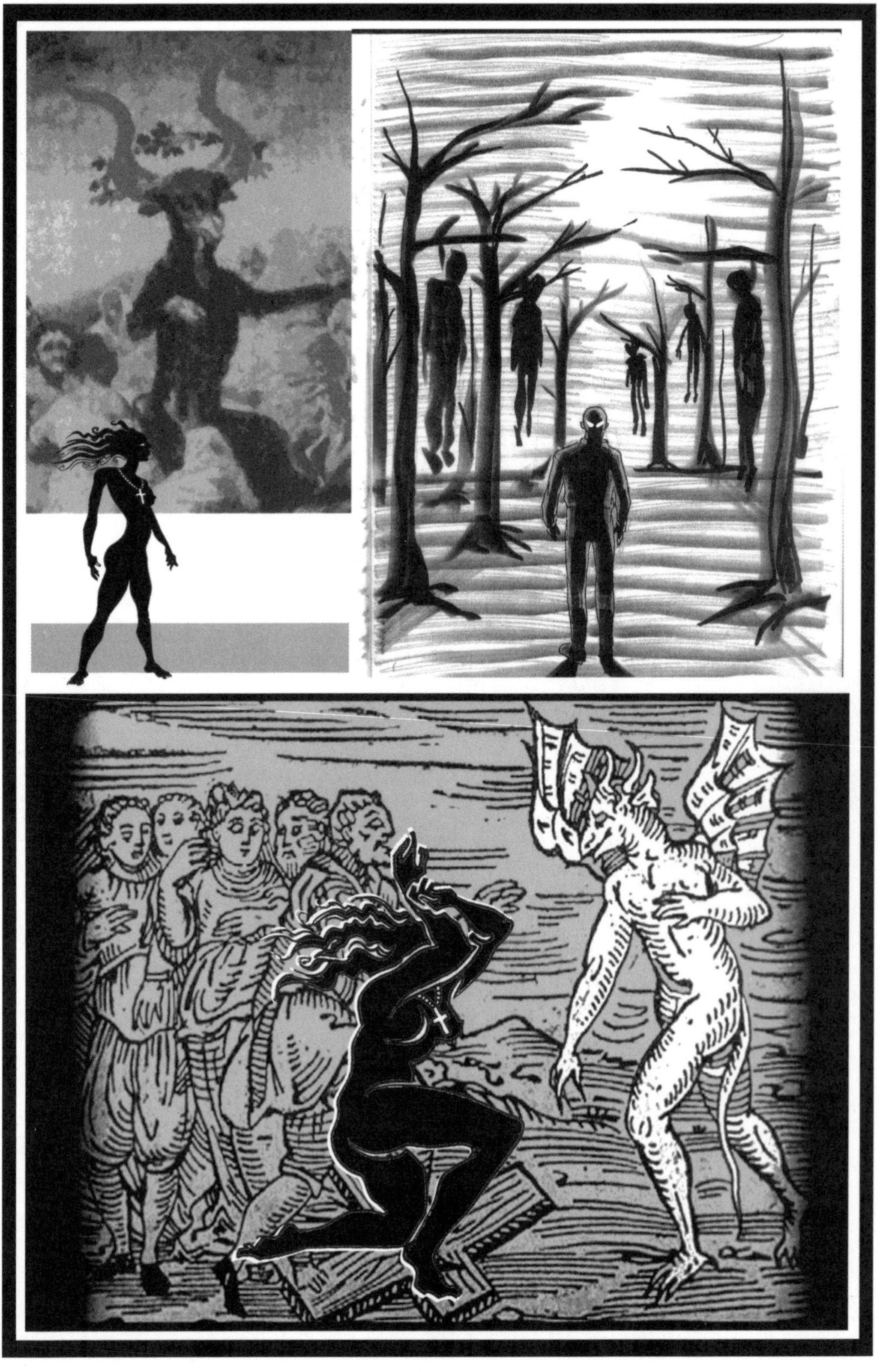

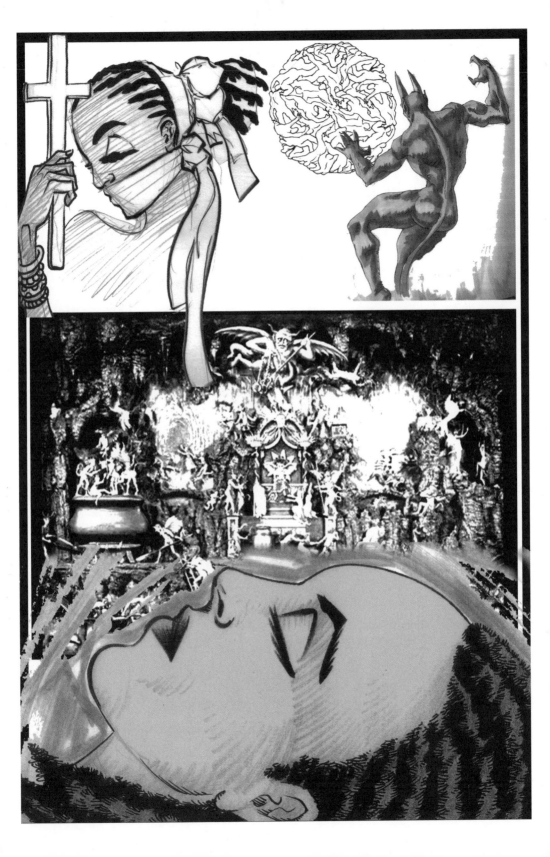

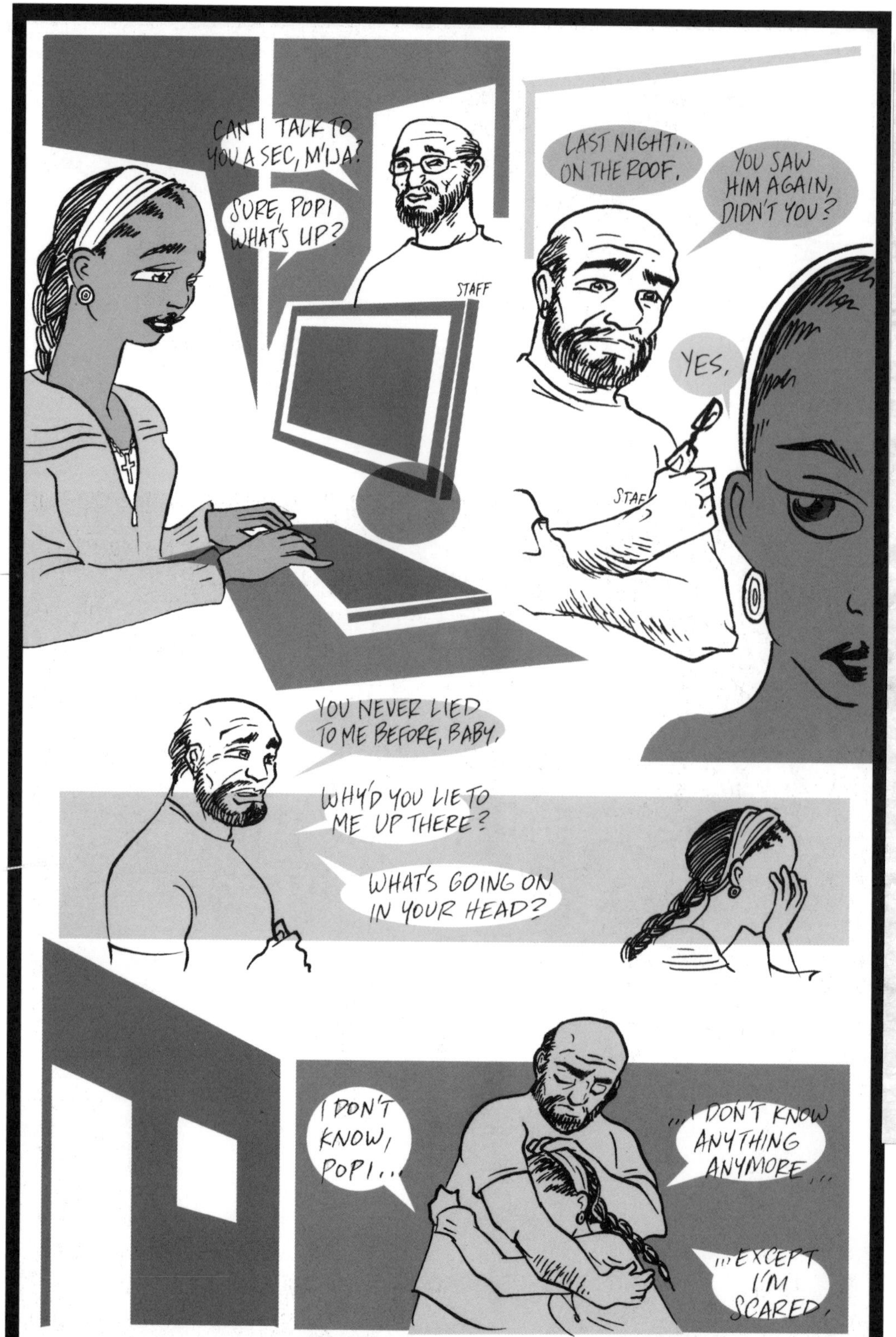

CAN I TALK TO YOU A SEC, M'IJA?
SURE, POPI WHAT'S UP?
STAFF
LAST NIGHT... ON THE ROOF.
YOU SAW HIM AGAIN, DIDN'T YOU?
YES.
STAF
YOU NEVER LIED TO ME BEFORE, BABY.
WHY'D YOU LIE TO ME UP THERE?
WHAT'S GOING ON IN YOUR HEAD?
I DON'T KNOW, POPI...
...I DON'T KNOW ANYTHING ANYMORE...
...EXCEPT I'M SCARED.

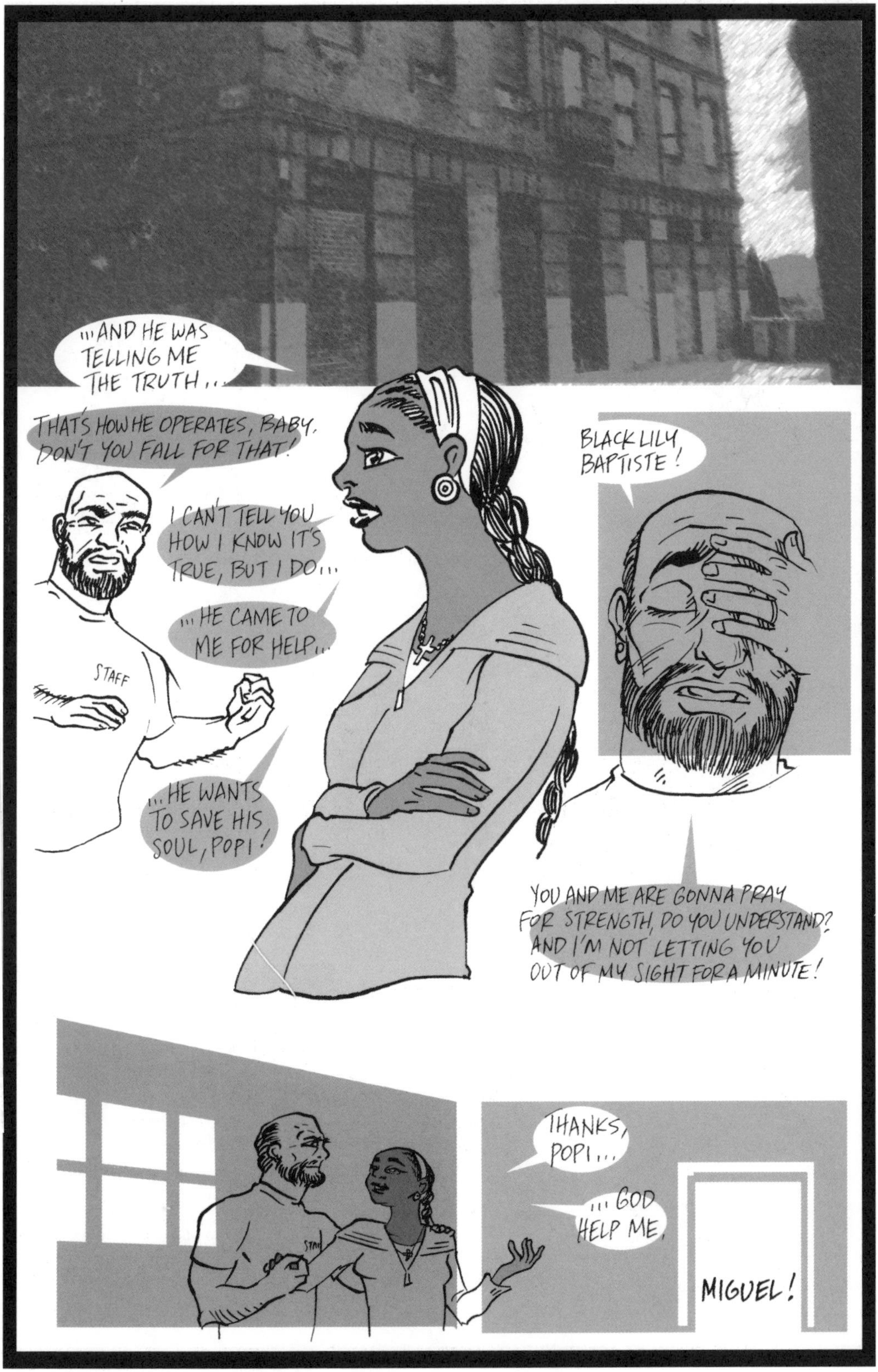
...AND HE WAS TELLING ME THE TRUTH...
THAT'S HOW HE OPERATES, BABY. DON'T YOU FALL FOR THAT!
I CAN'T TELL YOU HOW I KNOW IT'S TRUE, BUT I DO...
...HE CAME TO ME FOR HELP...
...HE WANTS TO SAVE HIS SOUL, POPI!
STAFF
BLACK LILY BAPTISTE!
YOU AND ME ARE GONNA PRAY FOR STRENGTH, DO YOU UNDERSTAND? AND I'M NOT LETTING YOU OUT OF MY SIGHT FOR A MINUTE!
THANKS, POPI...
...GOD HELP ME.
MIGUEL!

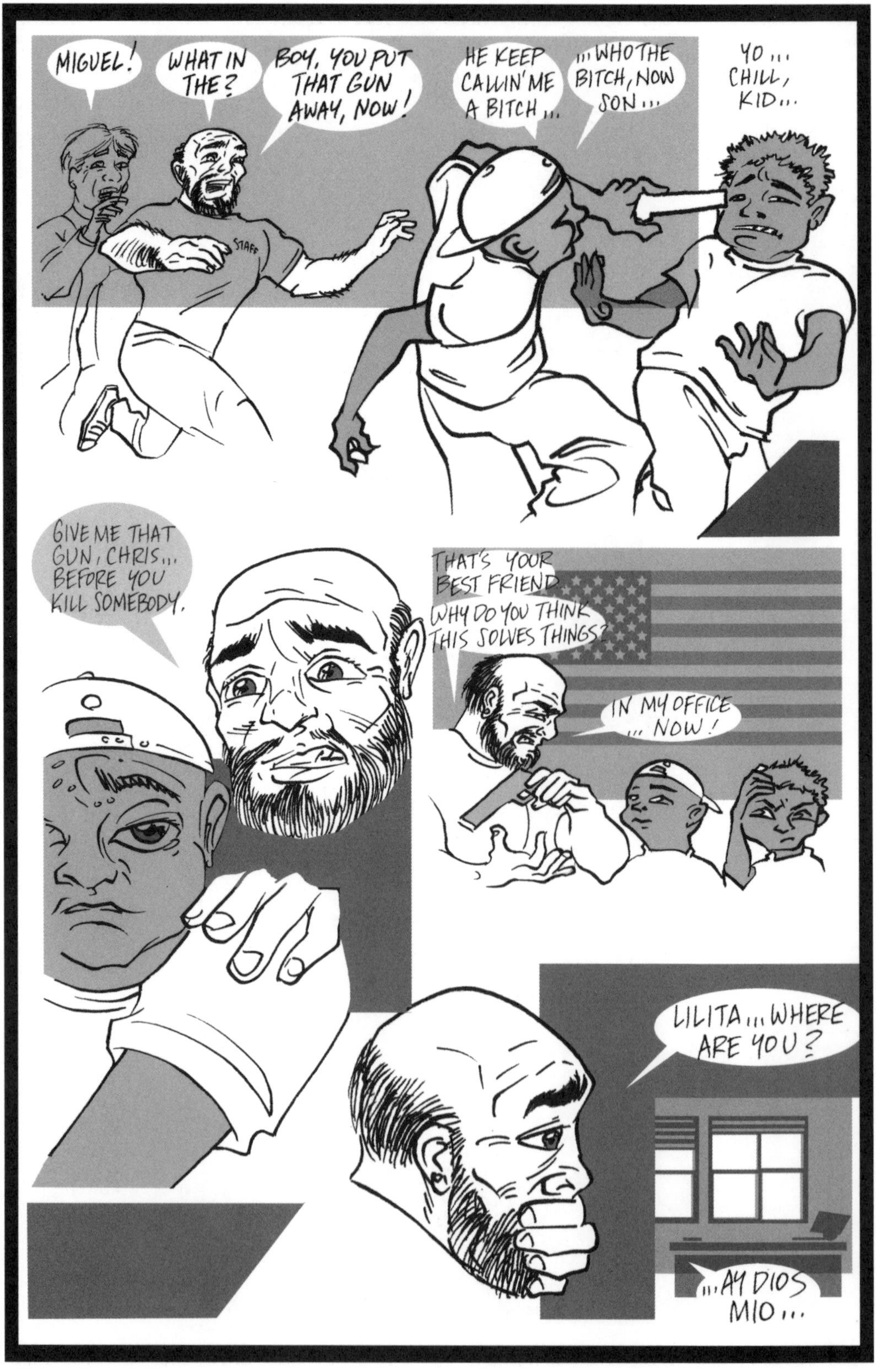
MIGUEL!
WHAT IN THE?
BOY, YOU PUT THAT GUN AWAY, NOW!
HE KEEP CALLIN' ME A BITCH...
...WHO THE BITCH, NOW SON...
YO... CHILL, KID...
GIVE ME THAT GUN, CHRIS... BEFORE YOU KILL SOMEBODY.
THAT'S YOUR BEST FRIEND. WHY DO YOU THINK THIS SOLVES THINGS?
IN MY OFFICE ... NOW!
LILITA... WHERE ARE YOU?
...AY DIOS MIO...

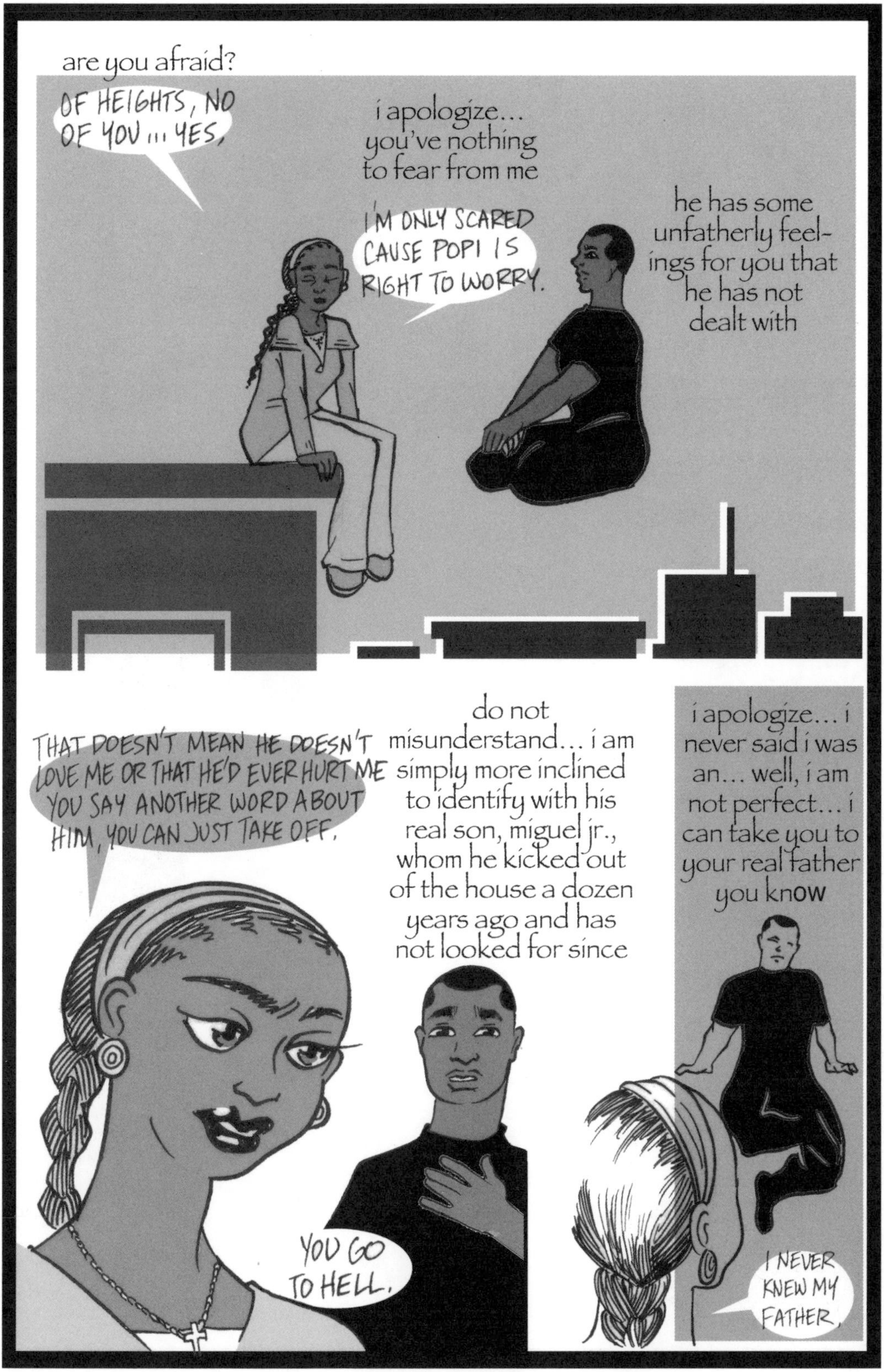
are you afraid?
OF HEIGHTS, NO OF YOU ... YES,
i apologize... you've nothing to fear from me
I'M ONLY SCARED CAUSE POPI IS RIGHT TO WORRY.
he has some unfatherly feelings for you that he has not dealt with
THAT DOESN'T MEAN HE DOESN'T LOVE ME OR THAT HE'D EVER HURT ME YOU SAY ANOTHER WORD ABOUT HIM, YOU CAN JUST TAKE OFF.
do not misunderstand... i am simply more inclined to identify with his real son, miguel jr., whom he kicked out of the house a dozen years ago and has not looked for since
YOU GO TO HELL.
i apologize... i never said i was an... well, i am not perfect... i can take you to your real father you know
I NEVER KNEW MY FATHER.

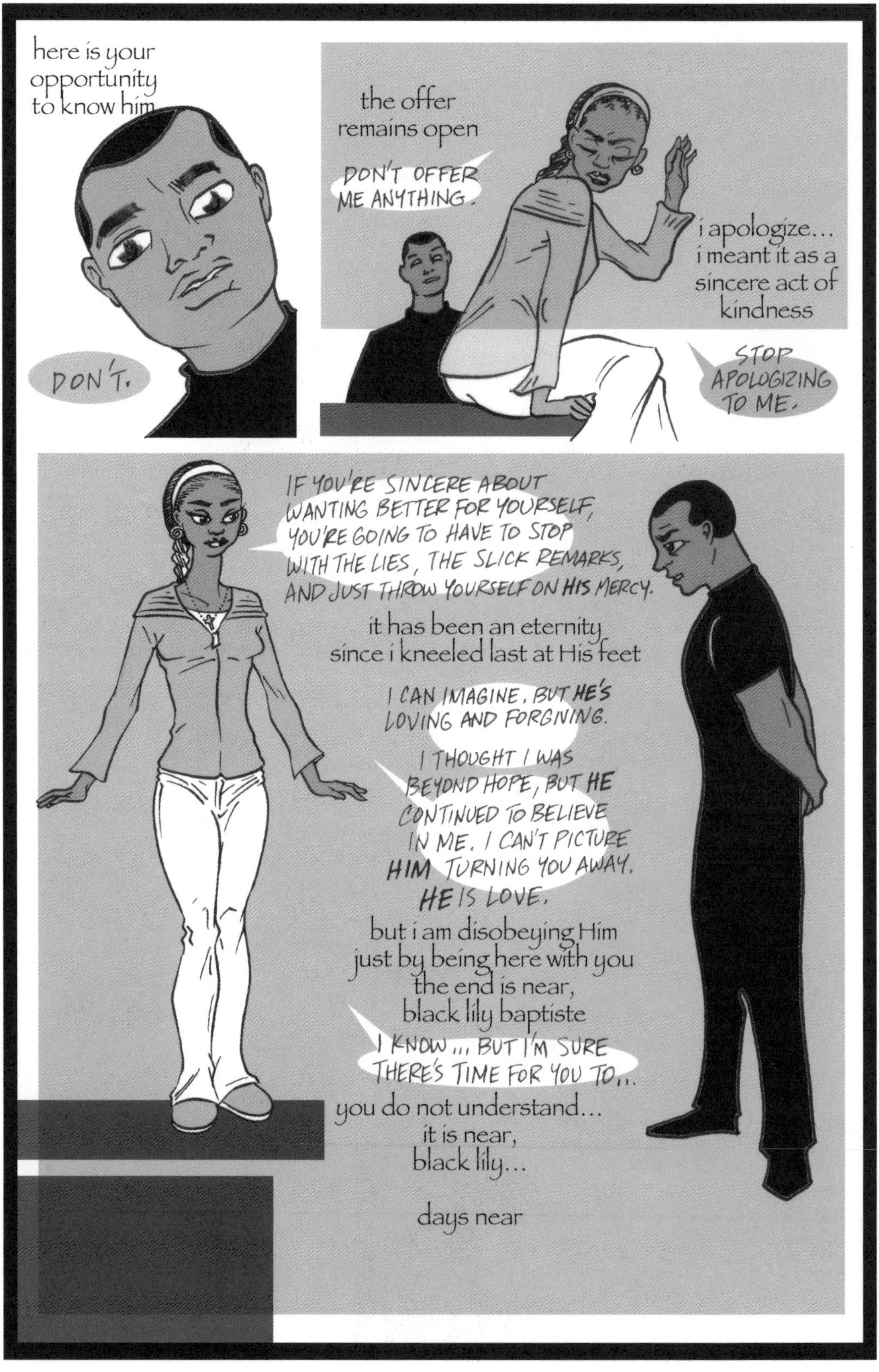
here is your opportunity to know him
DON'T.
the offer remains open
DON'T OFFER ME ANYTHING.
i apologize... i meant it as a sincere act of kindness
STOP APOLOGIZING TO ME.
IF YOU'RE SINCERE ABOUT WANTING BETTER FOR YOURSELF, YOU'RE GOING TO HAVE TO STOP WITH THE LIES, THE SLICK REMARKS, AND JUST THROW YOURSELF ON HIS MERCY.
it has been an eternity since i kneeled last at His feet
I CAN IMAGINE. BUT HE'S LOVING AND FORGIVING.
I THOUGHT I WAS BEYOND HOPE, BUT HE CONTINUED TO BELIEVE IN ME. I CAN'T PICTURE HIM TURNING YOU AWAY. HE IS LOVE.
but i am disobeying Him just by being here with you
the end is near, black lily baptiste
I KNOW... BUT I'M SURE THERE'S TIME FOR YOU TO...
you do not understand... it is near, black lily...
days near

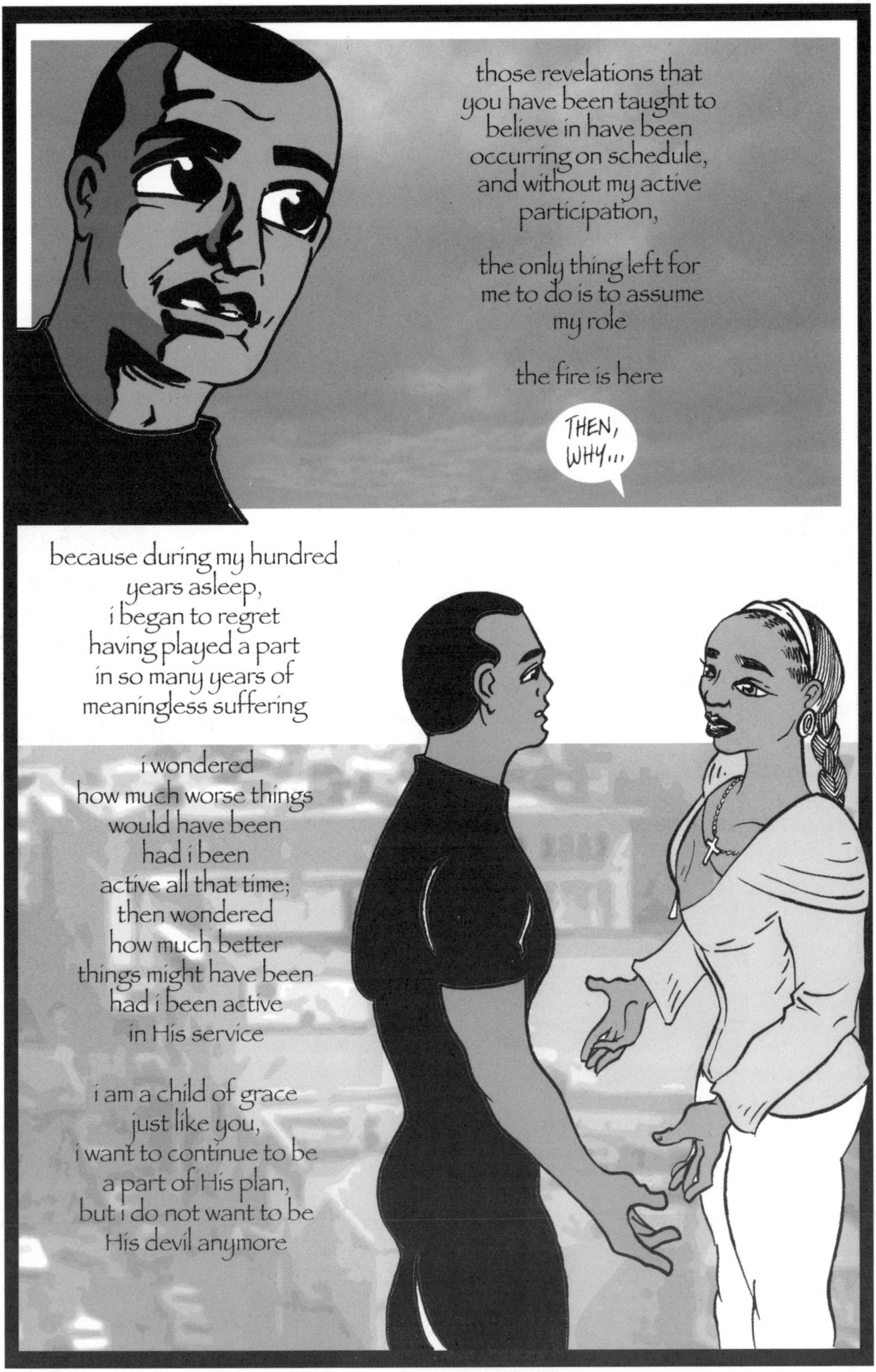
those revelations that you have been taught to believe in have been occurring on schedule, and without my active participation,
the only thing left for me to do is to assume my role
the fire is here
THEN, WHY...
because during my hundred years asleep, i began to regret having played a part in so many years of meaningless suffering
i wondered how much worse things would have been had i been active all that time; then wondered how much better things might have been had i been active in His service
i am a child of grace just like you, i want to continue to be a part of His plan, but i do not want to be His devil anymore

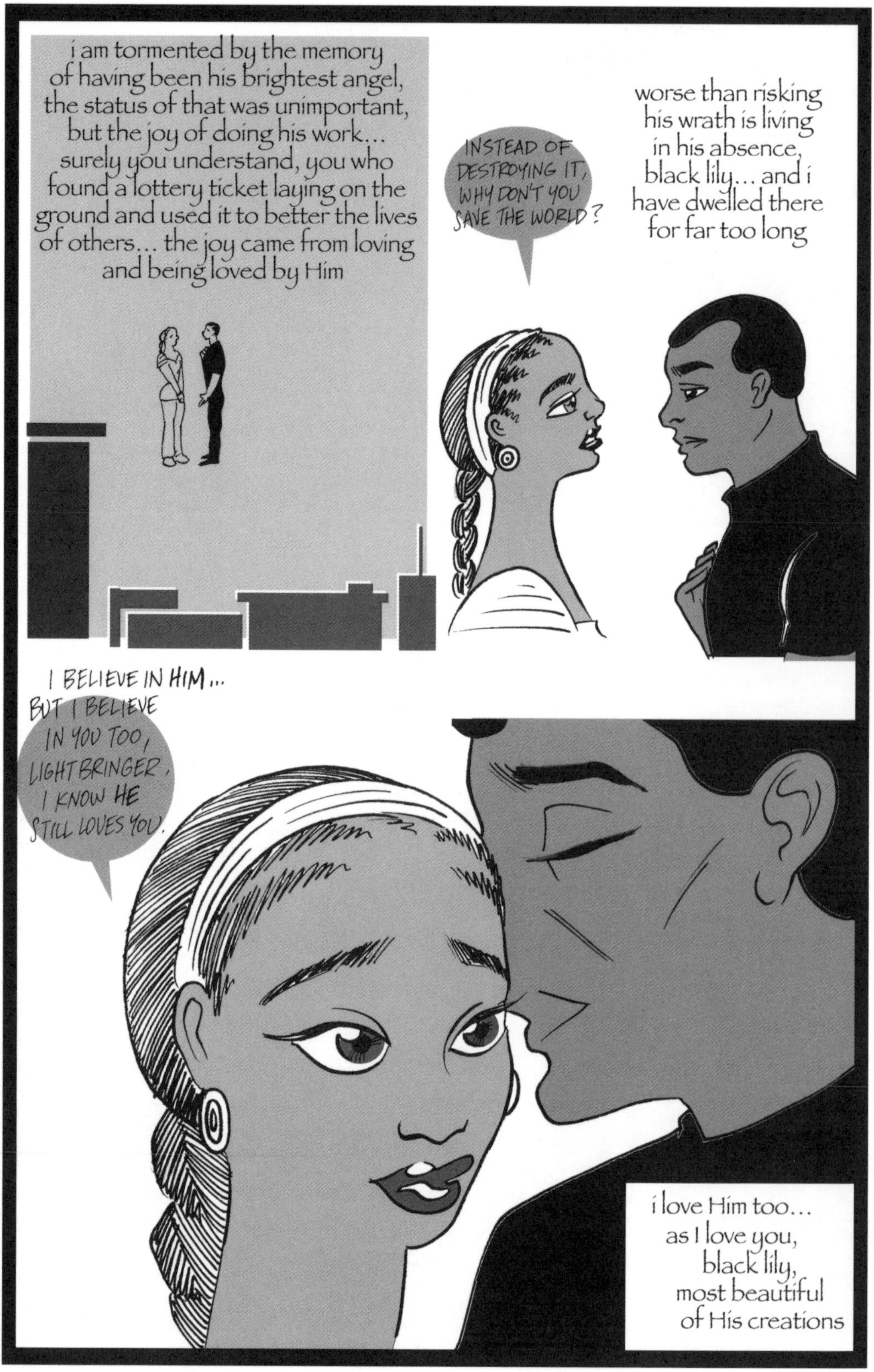
i am tormented by the memory of having been his brightest angel, the status of that was unimportant, but the joy of doing his work... surely you understand, you who found a lottery ticket laying on the ground and used it to better the lives of others... the joy came from loving and being loved by Him
INSTEAD OF DESTROYING IT, WHY DON'T YOU SAVE THE WORLD?
worse than risking his wrath is living in his absence, black lily... and i have dwelled there for far too long
I BELIEVE IN HIM... BUT I BELIEVE IN YOU TOO, LIGHTBRINGER, I KNOW HE STILL LOVES YOU.
i love Him too... as I love you, black lily, most beautiful of His creations

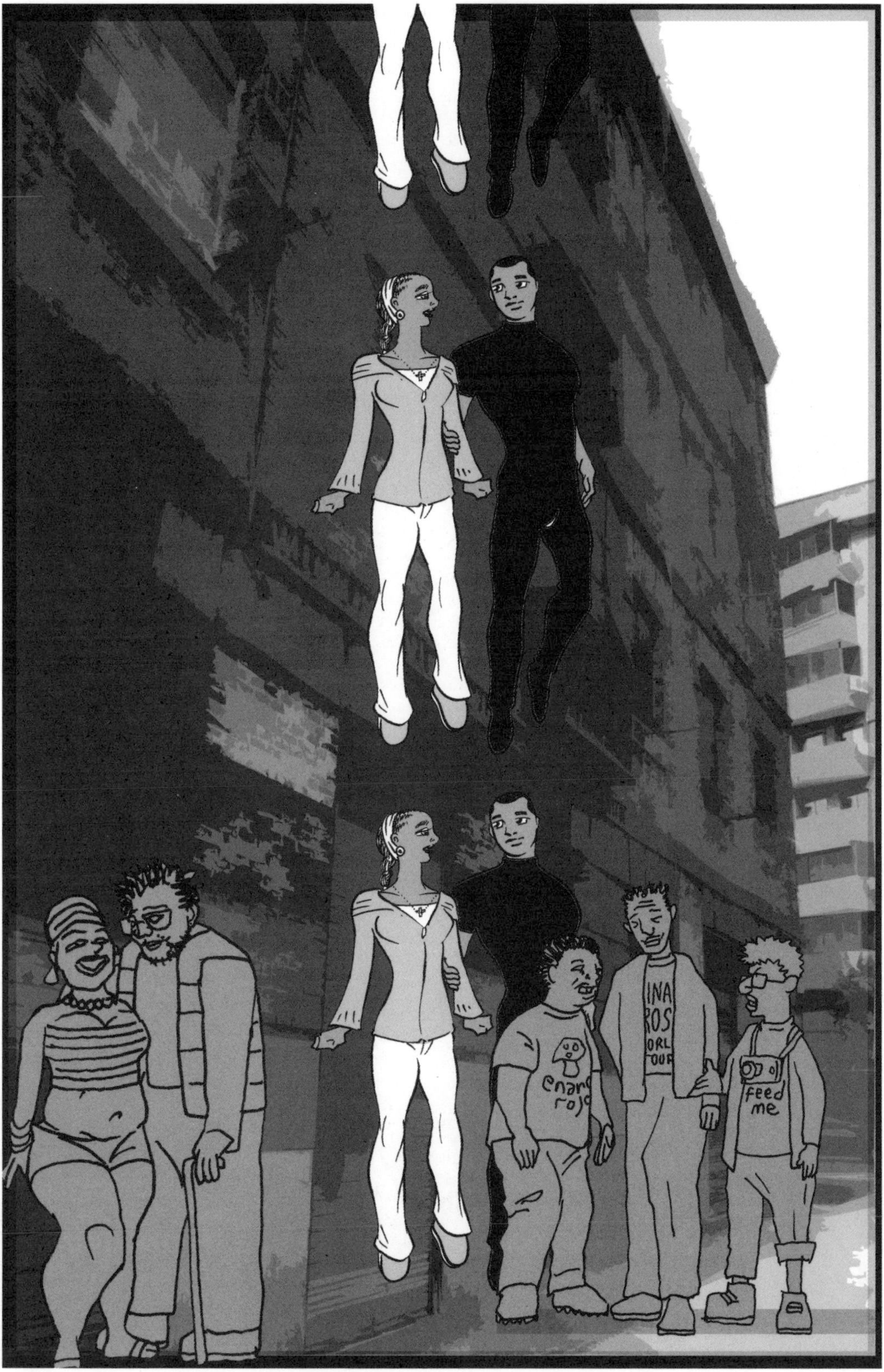

feed me

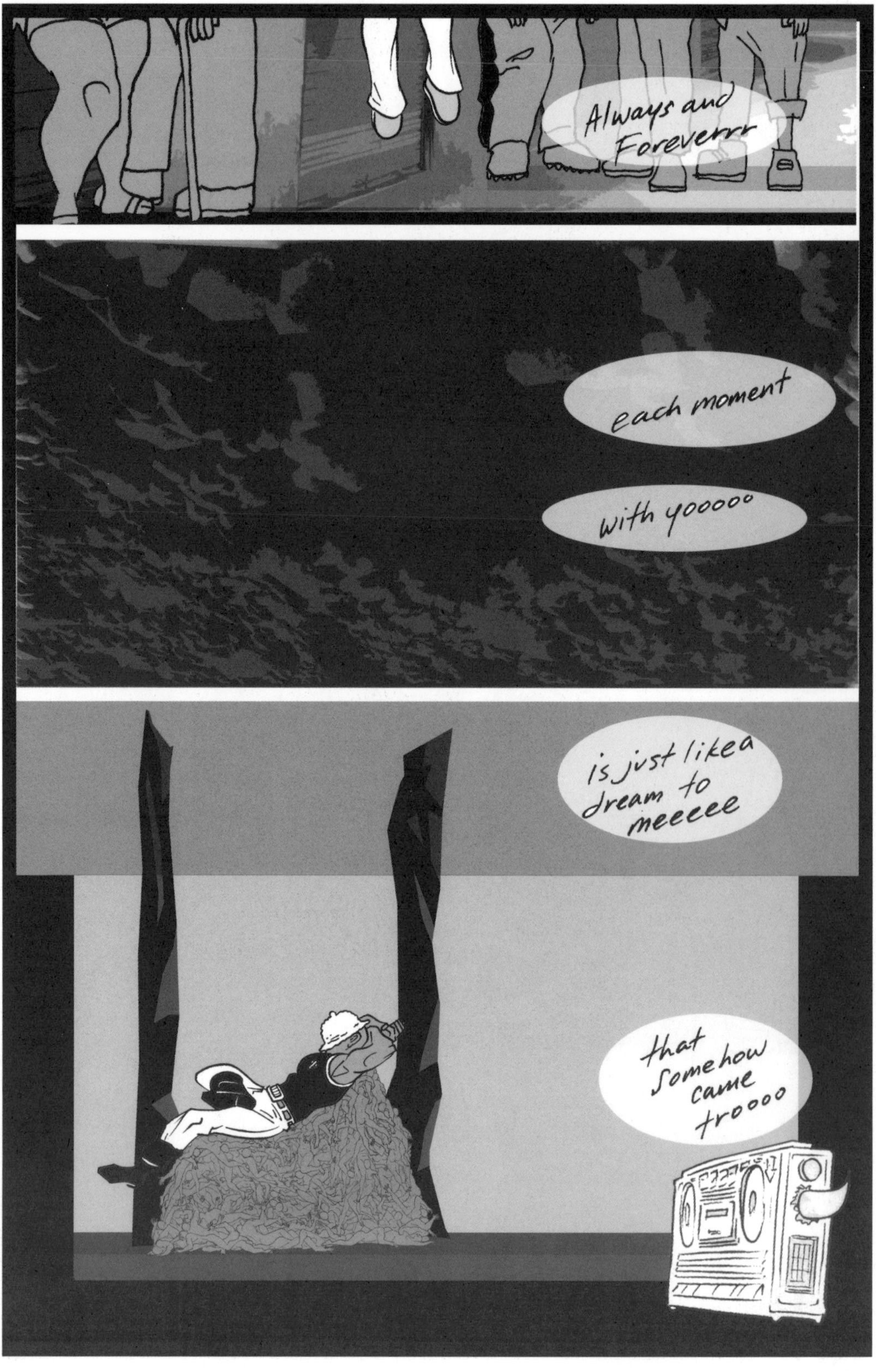
Always and Foreverrr
each moment
with yooooo
is just likea dream to meeeee
that Somehow came troooo

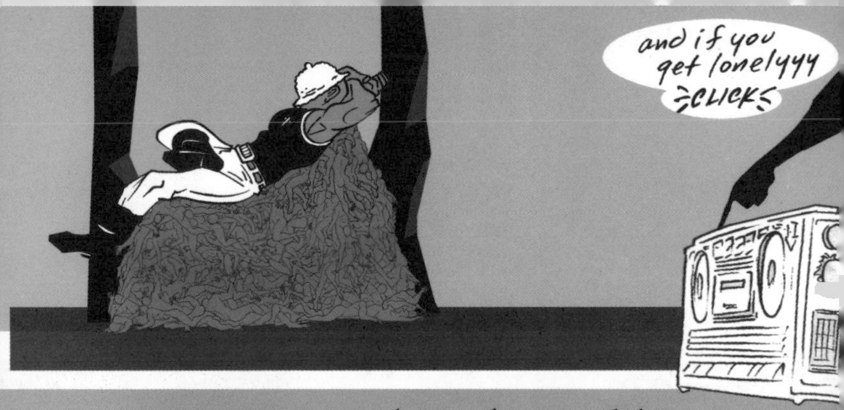
and if you get lonelyyy
CLICK

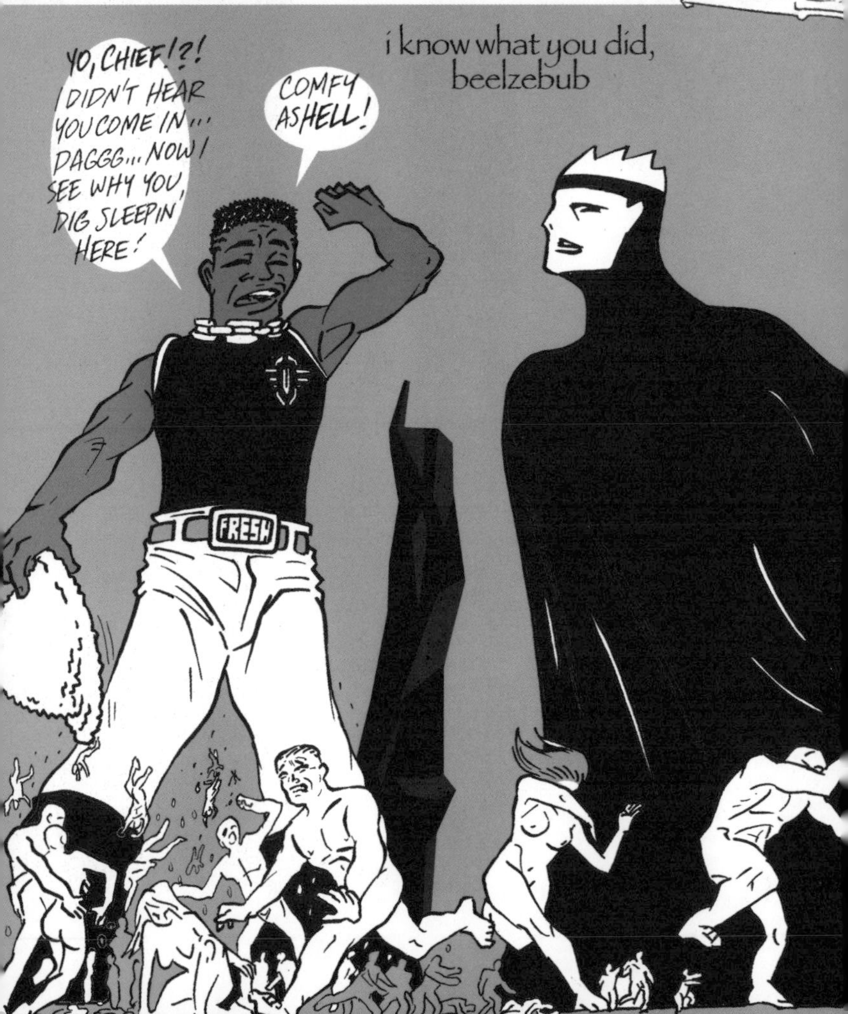
i know what you did, beelzebub
YO, CHIEF!?! I DIDN'T HEAR YOU COME IN... DAGGG... NOW I SEE WHY YOU DIG SLEEPIN' HERE!
COMFY AS HELL!
FRESH

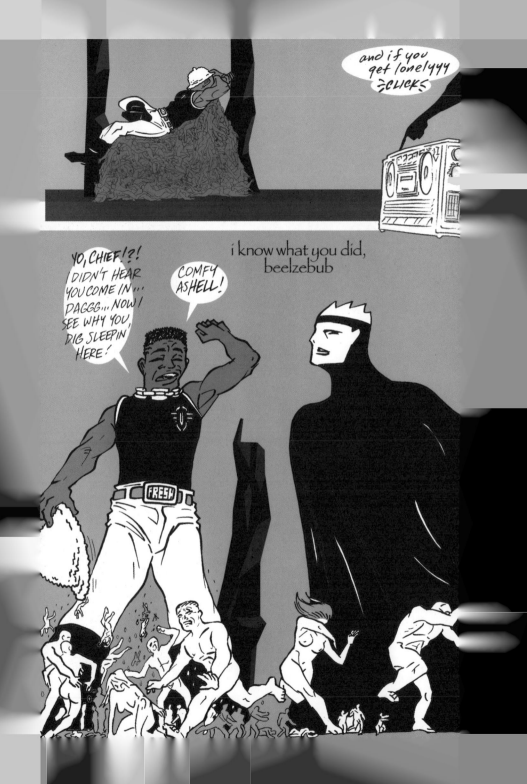

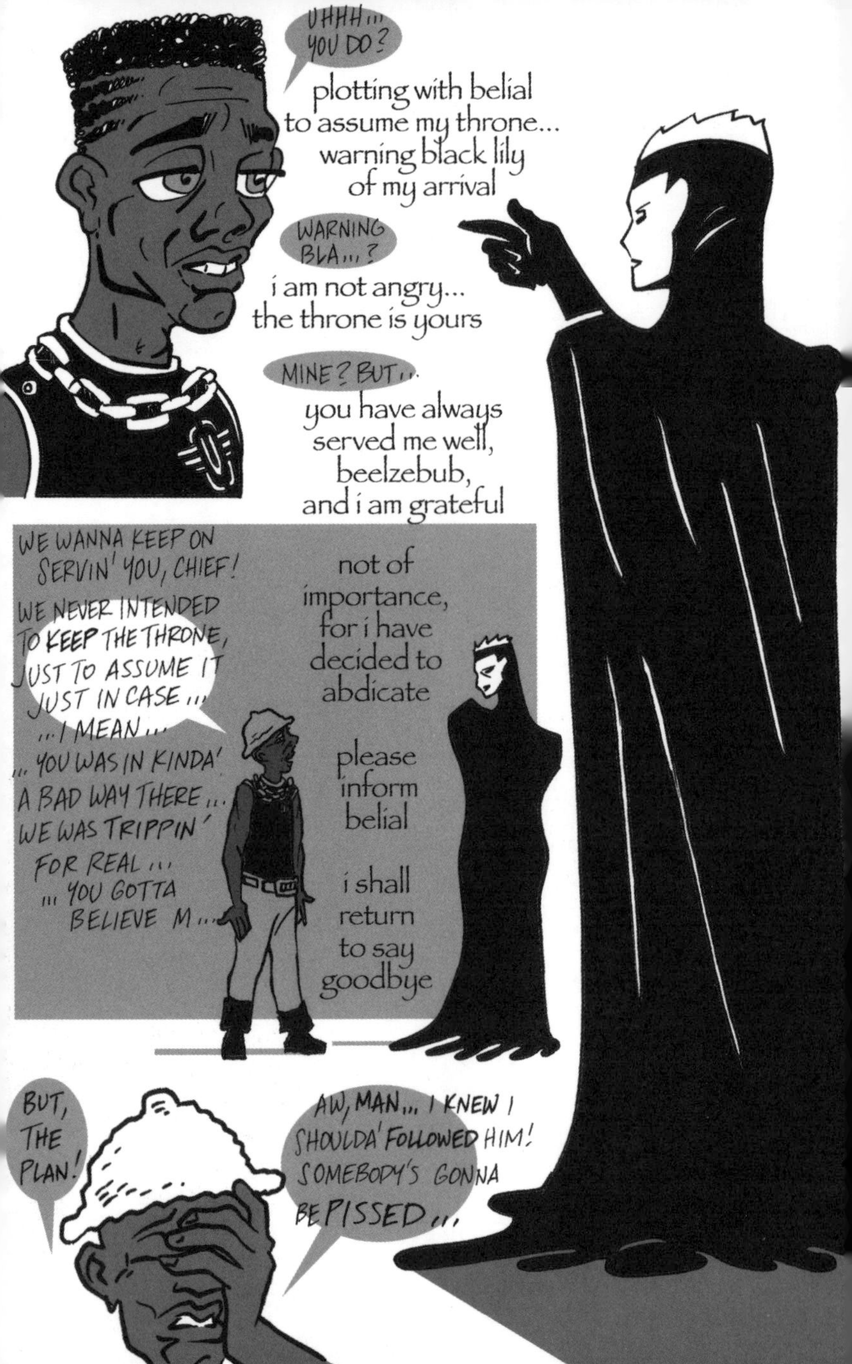
UHHH... YOU DO?
plotting with belial to assume my throne... warning black lily of my arrival
WARNING BLA...?
i am not angry... the throne is yours
MINE? BUT...
you have always served me well, beelzebub, and i am grateful
WE WANNA KEEP ON SERVIN' YOU, CHIEF! WE NEVER INTENDED TO KEEP THE THRONE, JUST TO ASSUME IT JUST IN CASE... ...I MEAN... ...YOU WAS IN KINDA' A BAD WAY THERE... WE WAS TRIPPIN' FOR REAL... ...YOU GOTTA BELIEVE M...
not of importance, for i have decided to abdicate
please inform belial
i shall return to say goodbye
BUT, THE PLAN!
AW, MAN... I KNEW I SHOULDA' FOLLOWED HIM! SOMEBODY'S GONNA BE PISSED...

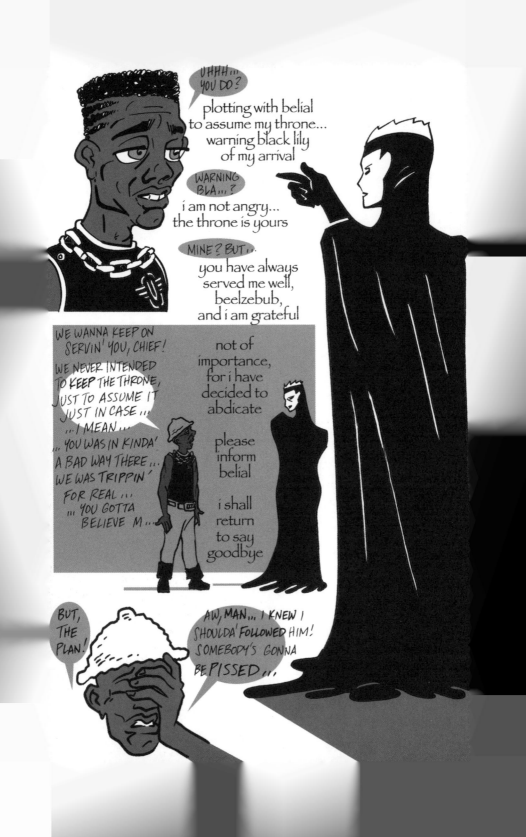

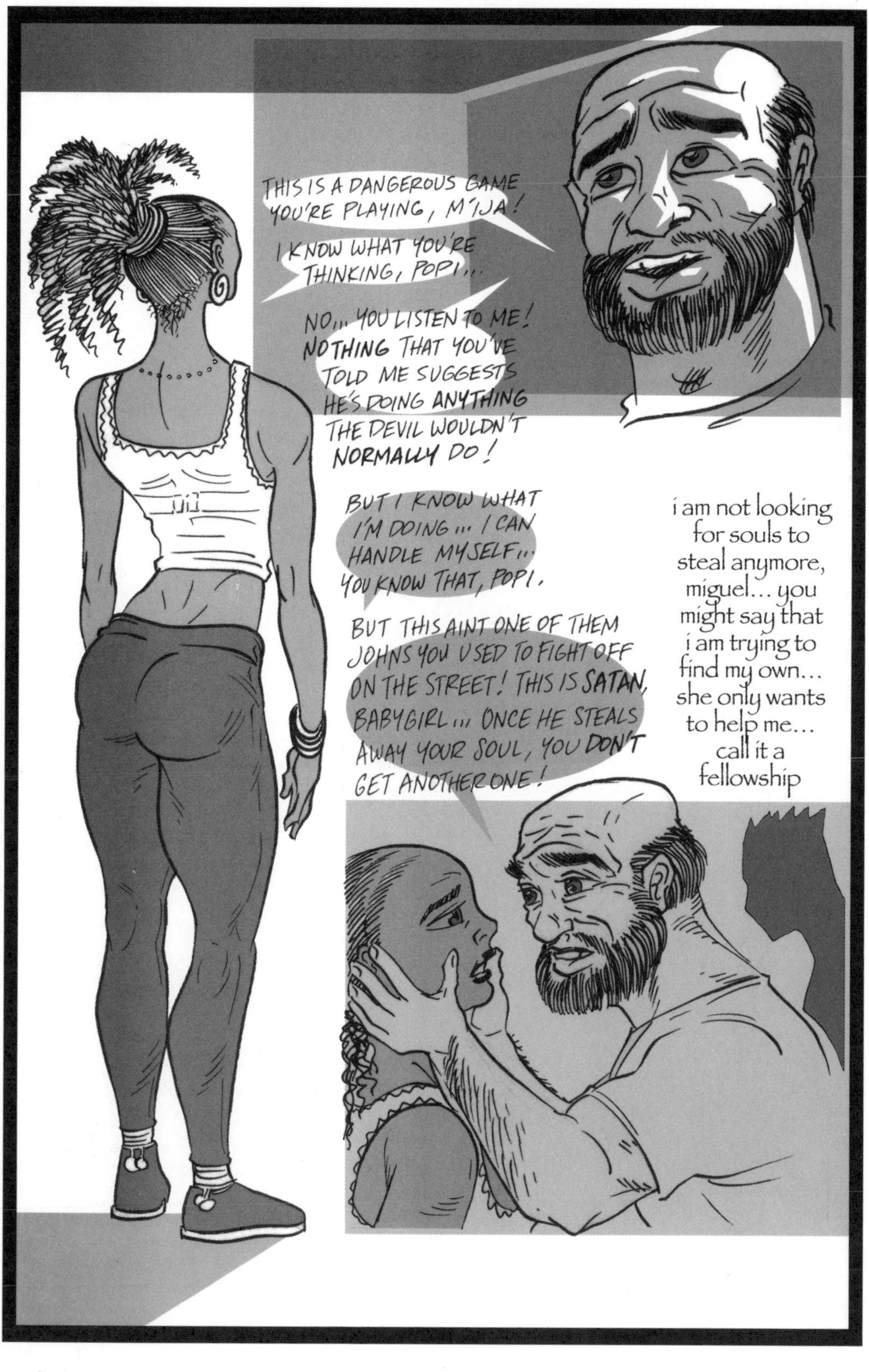
THIS IS A DANGEROUS GAME YOU'RE PLAYING, M'IJA!
I KNOW WHAT YOU'RE THINKING, POPI...
NO... YOU LISTEN TO ME! NOTHING THAT YOU'VE TOLD ME SUGGESTS HE'S DOING ANYTHING THE DEVIL WOULDN'T NORMALLY DO!
BUT I KNOW WHAT I'M DOING... I CAN HANDLE MYSELF... YOU KNOW THAT, POPI.
BUT THIS AINT ONE OF THEM JOHNS YOU USED TO FIGHT OFF ON THE STREET! THIS IS SATAN, BABYGIRL... ONCE HE STEALS AWAY YOUR SOUL, YOU DON'T GET ANOTHER ONE!
i am not looking for souls to steal anymore, miguel... you might say that i am trying to find my own... she only wants to help me... call it a fellowship

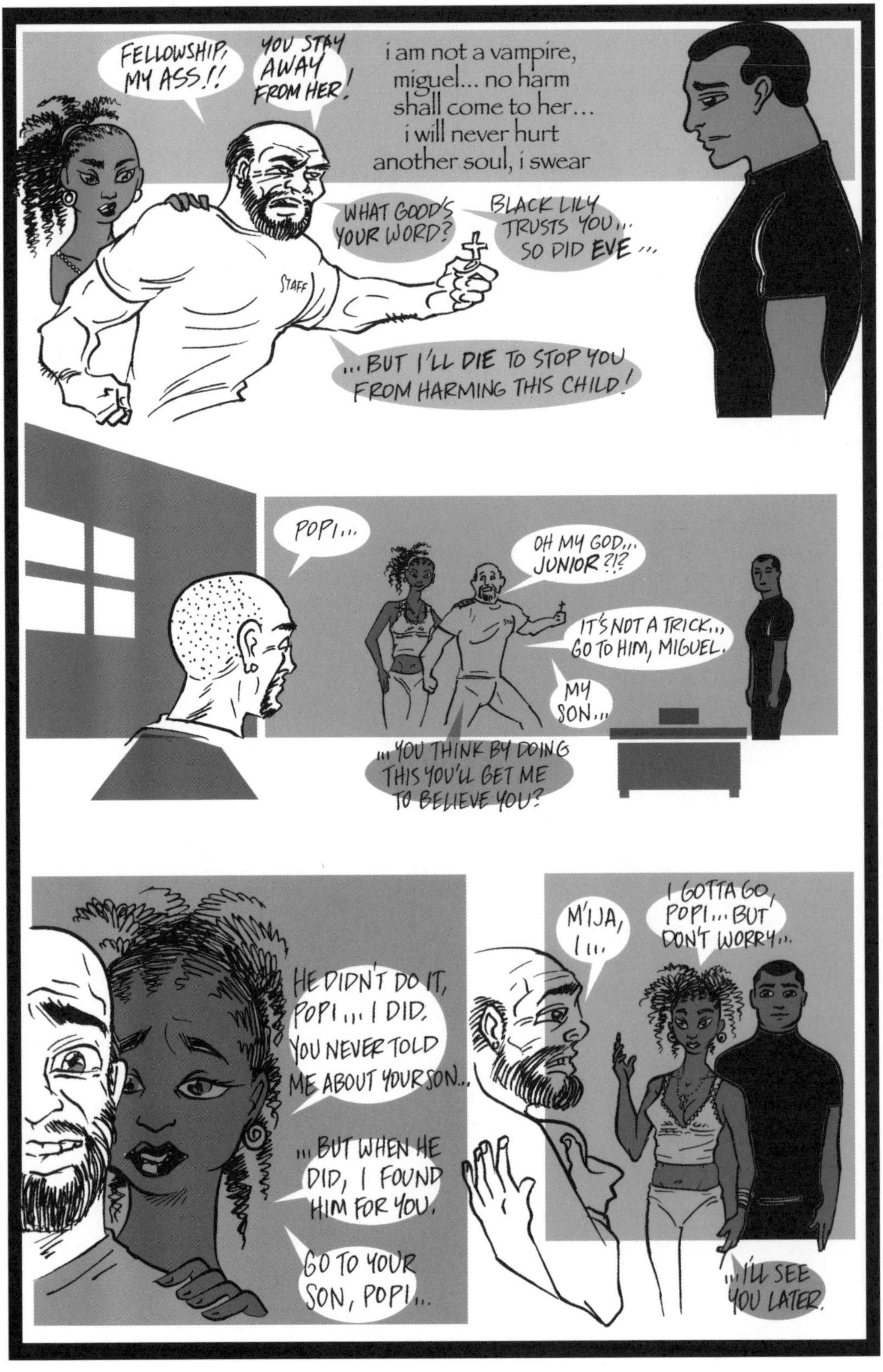
FELLOWSHIP, MY ASS!!
YOU STAY AWAY FROM HER!
i am not a vampire, miguel... no harm shall come to her... i will never hurt another soul, i swear
WHAT GOOD'S YOUR WORD?
BLACK LILY TRUSTS YOU... SO DID EVE...
...BUT I'LL DIE TO STOP YOU FROM HARMING THIS CHILD!
POPI...
OH MY GOD... JUNIOR?!?
IT'S NOT A TRICK... GO TO HIM, MIGUEL.
MY SON...
...YOU THINK BY DOING THIS YOU'LL GET ME TO BELIEVE YOU?
HE DIDN'T DO IT, POPI... I DID. YOU NEVER TOLD ME ABOUT YOUR SON...
...BUT WHEN HE DID, I FOUND HIM FOR YOU.
GO TO YOUR SON, POPI...
M'IJA, I...
I GOTTA GO, POPI... BUT DON'T WORRY...
...I'LL SEE YOU LATER.

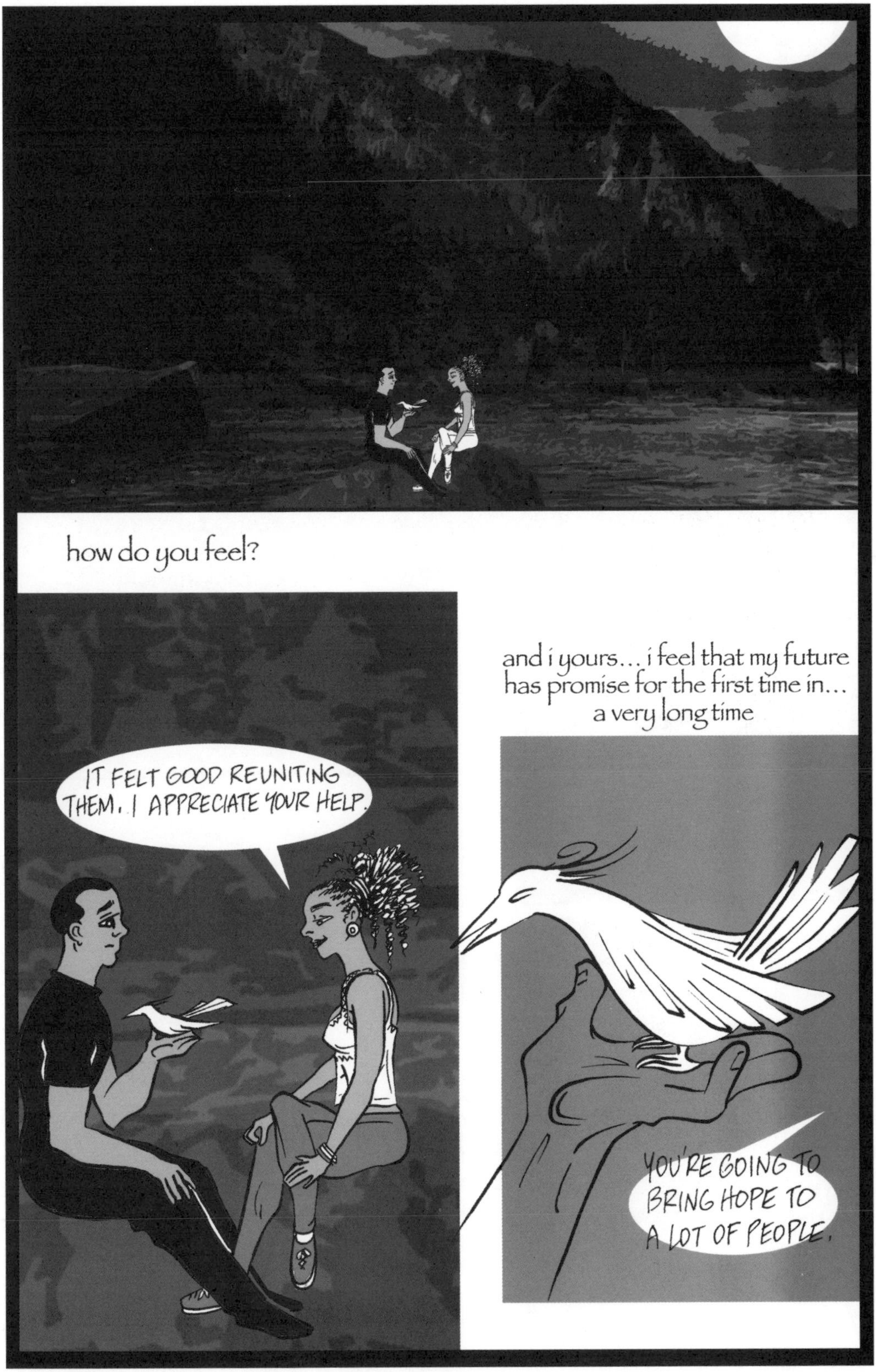
how do you feel?
IT FELT GOOD REUNITING THEM. I APPRECIATE YOUR HELP.
and i yours... i feel that my future has promise for the first time in... a very long time
YOU'RE GOING TO BRING HOPE TO A LOT OF PEOPLE.

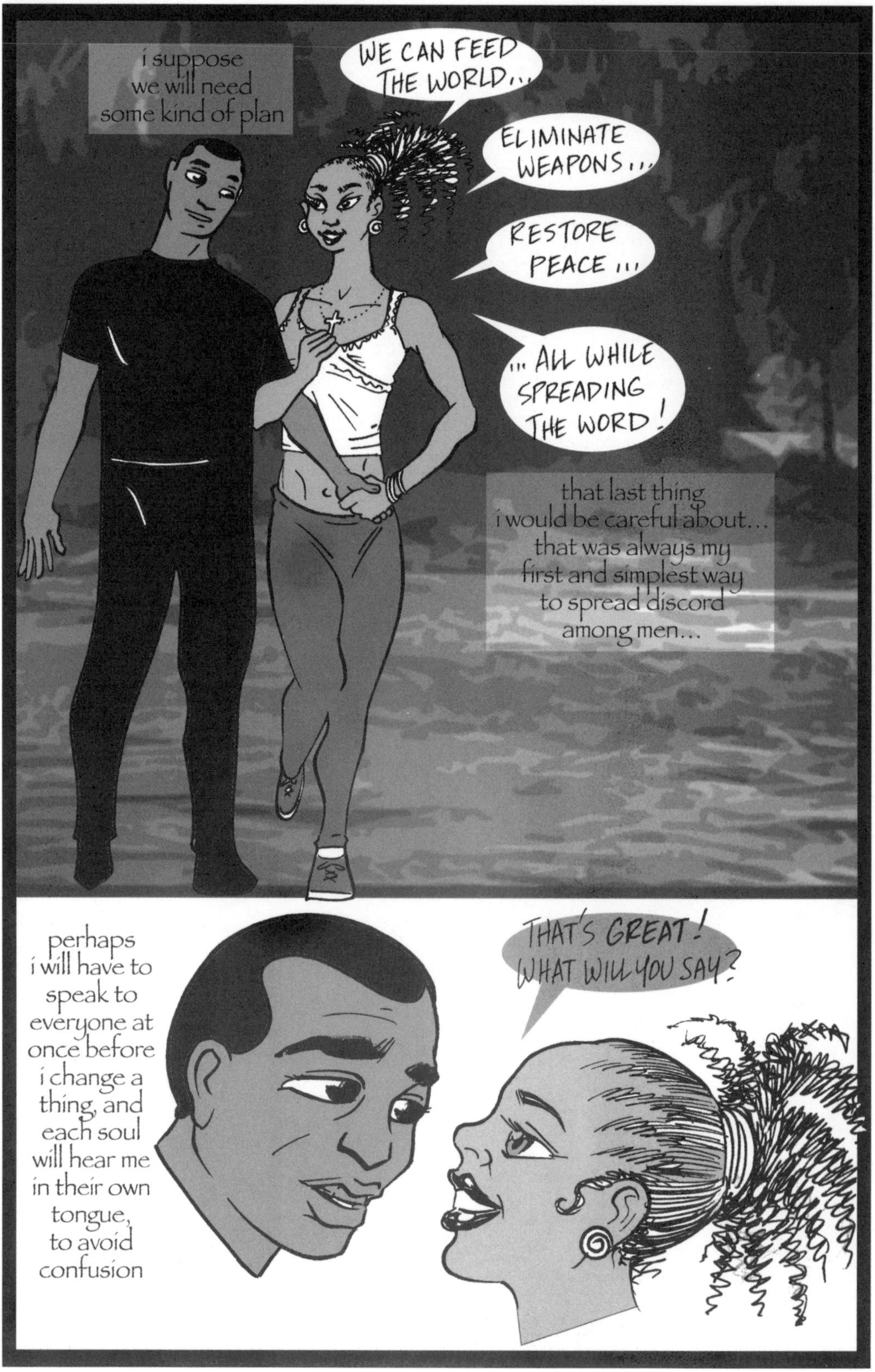

i suppose we will need some kind of plan
WE CAN FEED THE WORLD...
ELIMINATE WEAPONS...
RESTORE PEACE...
... ALL WHILE SPREADING THE WORD!
that last thing i would be careful about... that was always my first and simplest way to spread discord among men...
perhaps i will have to speak to everyone at once before i change a thing, and each soul will hear me in their own tongue, to avoid confusion
THAT'S GREAT! WHAT WILL YOU SAY?

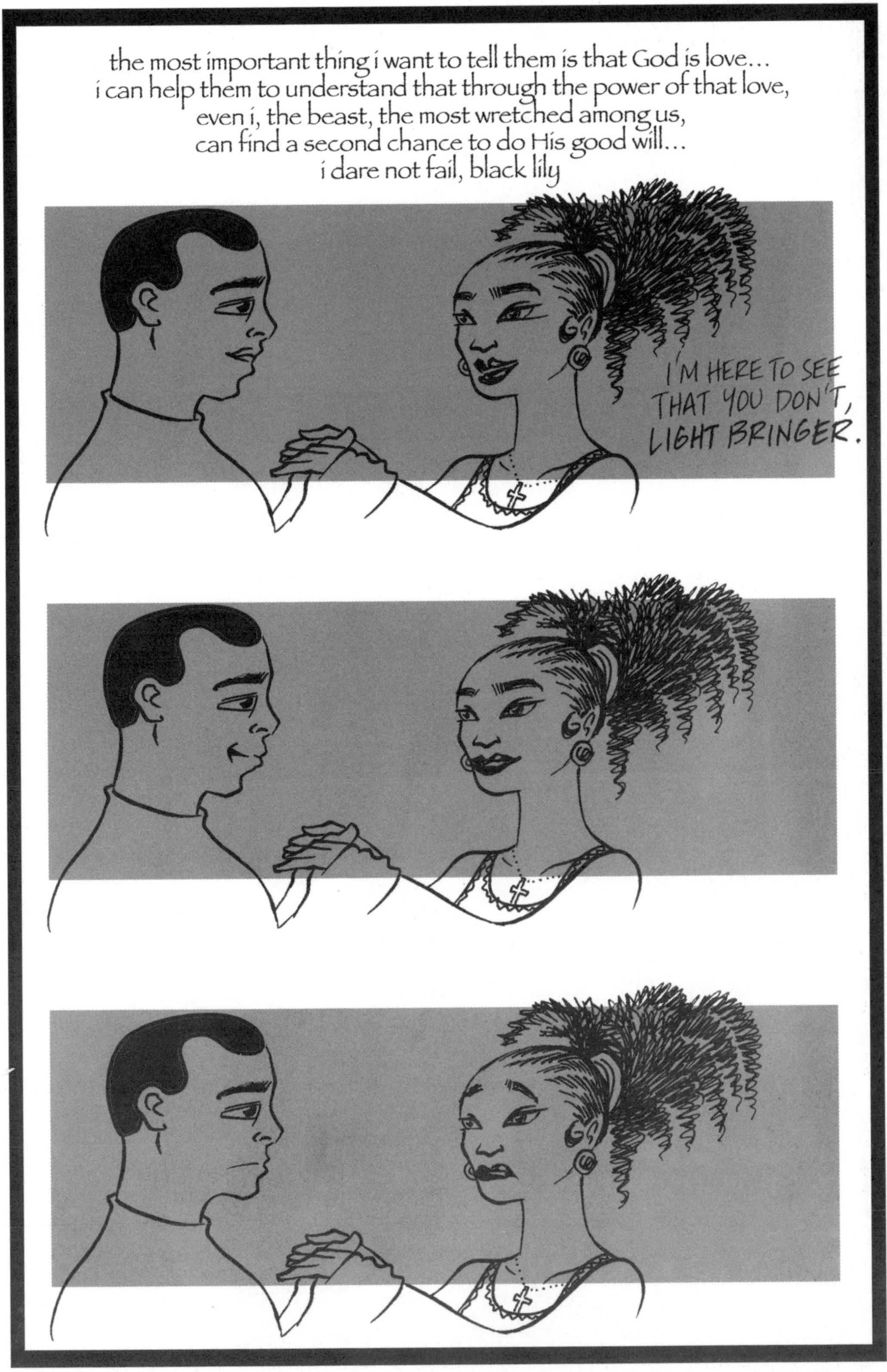
the most important thing i want to tell them is that God is love...
i can help them to understand that through the power of that love,
even i, the beast, the most wretched among us,
can find a second chance to do His good will...
i dare not fail, black lily
I'M HERE TO SEE THAT YOU DON'T, LIGHT BRINGER.

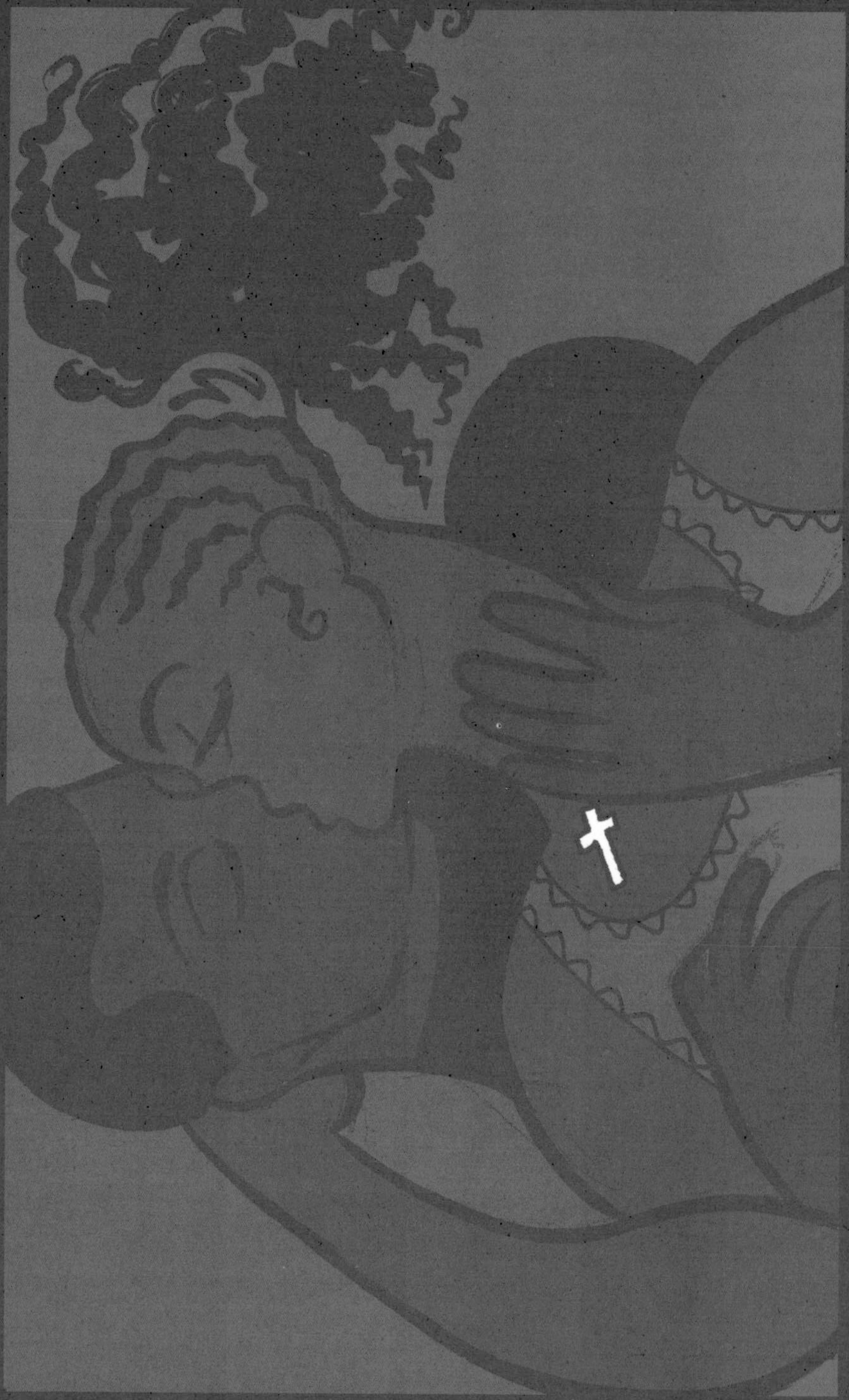

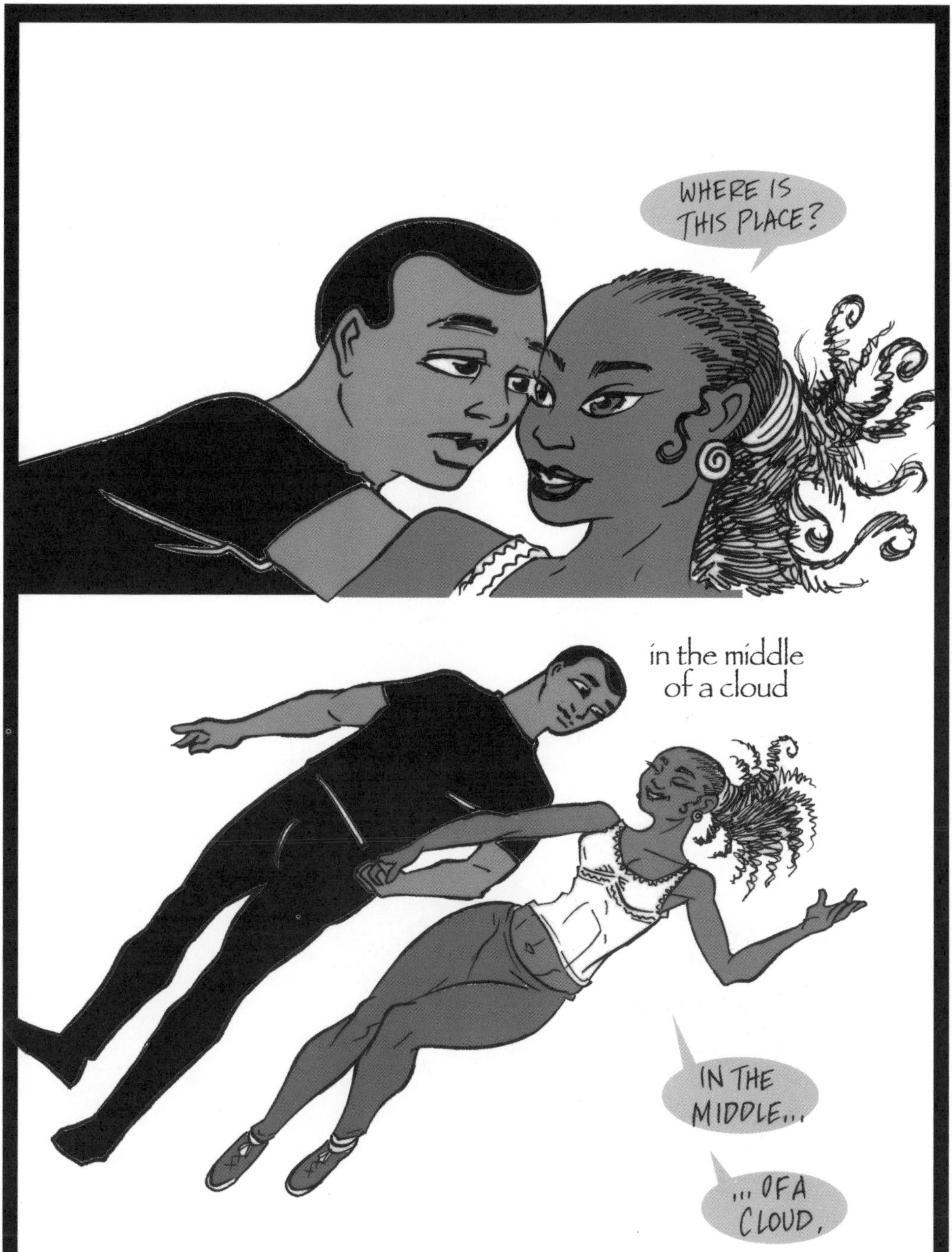
WHERE IS THIS PLACE?
in the middle of a cloud
IN THE MIDDLE...
... OF A CLOUD.
NO WAY, MAN.

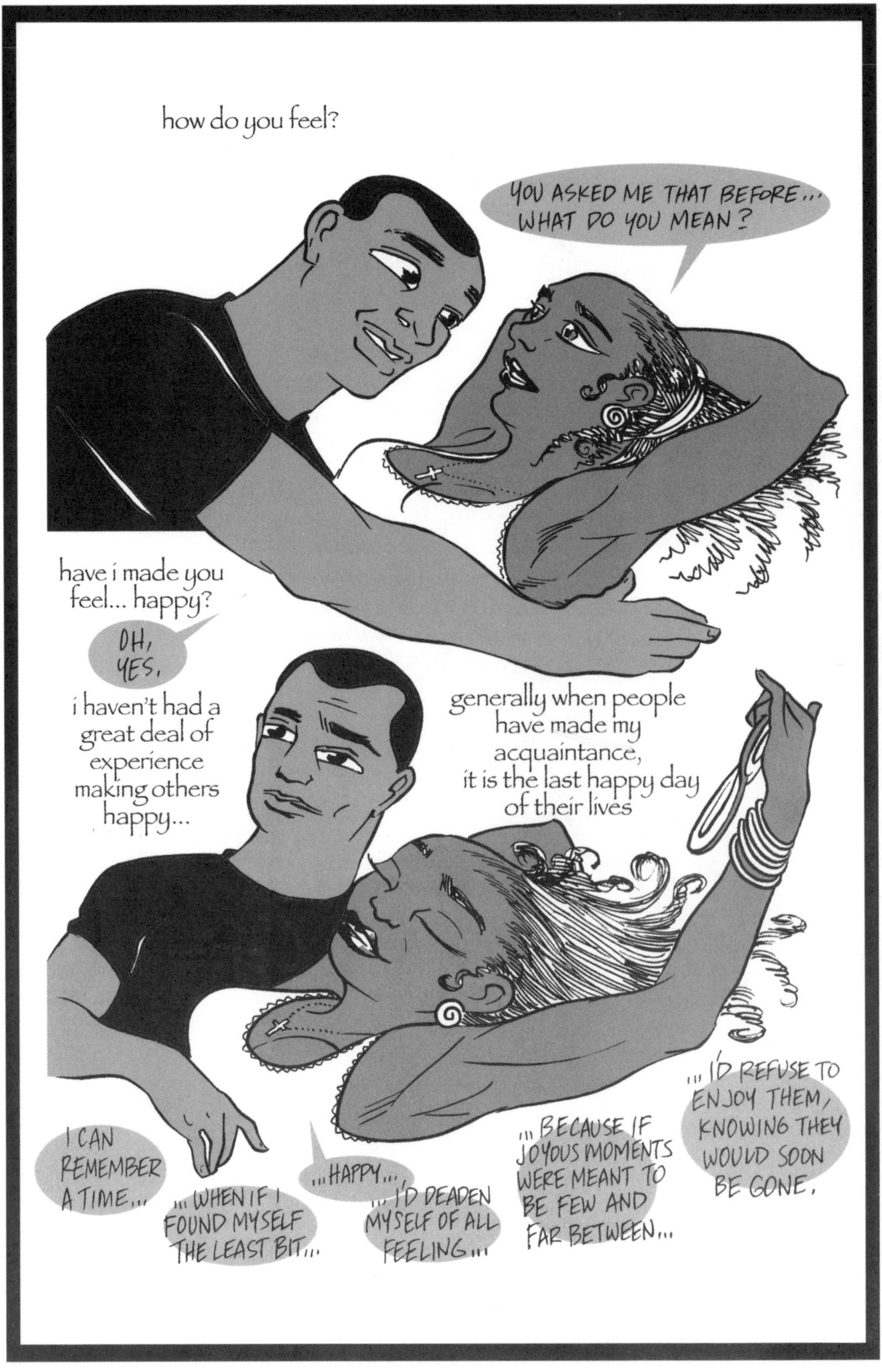
how do you feel?
YOU ASKED ME THAT BEFORE... WHAT DO YOU MEAN?
have i made you feel... happy?
OH, YES.
i haven't had a great deal of experience making others happy...
generally when people have made my acquaintance, it is the last happy day of their lives
I CAN REMEMBER A TIME...
...WHEN IF I FOUND MYSELF THE LEAST BIT...
...HAPPY...
...I'D DEADEN MYSELF OF ALL FEELING...
...BECAUSE IF JOYOUS MOMENTS WERE MEANT TO BE FEW AND FAR BETWEEN...
...I'D REFUSE TO ENJOY THEM, KNOWING THEY WOULD SOON BE GONE.

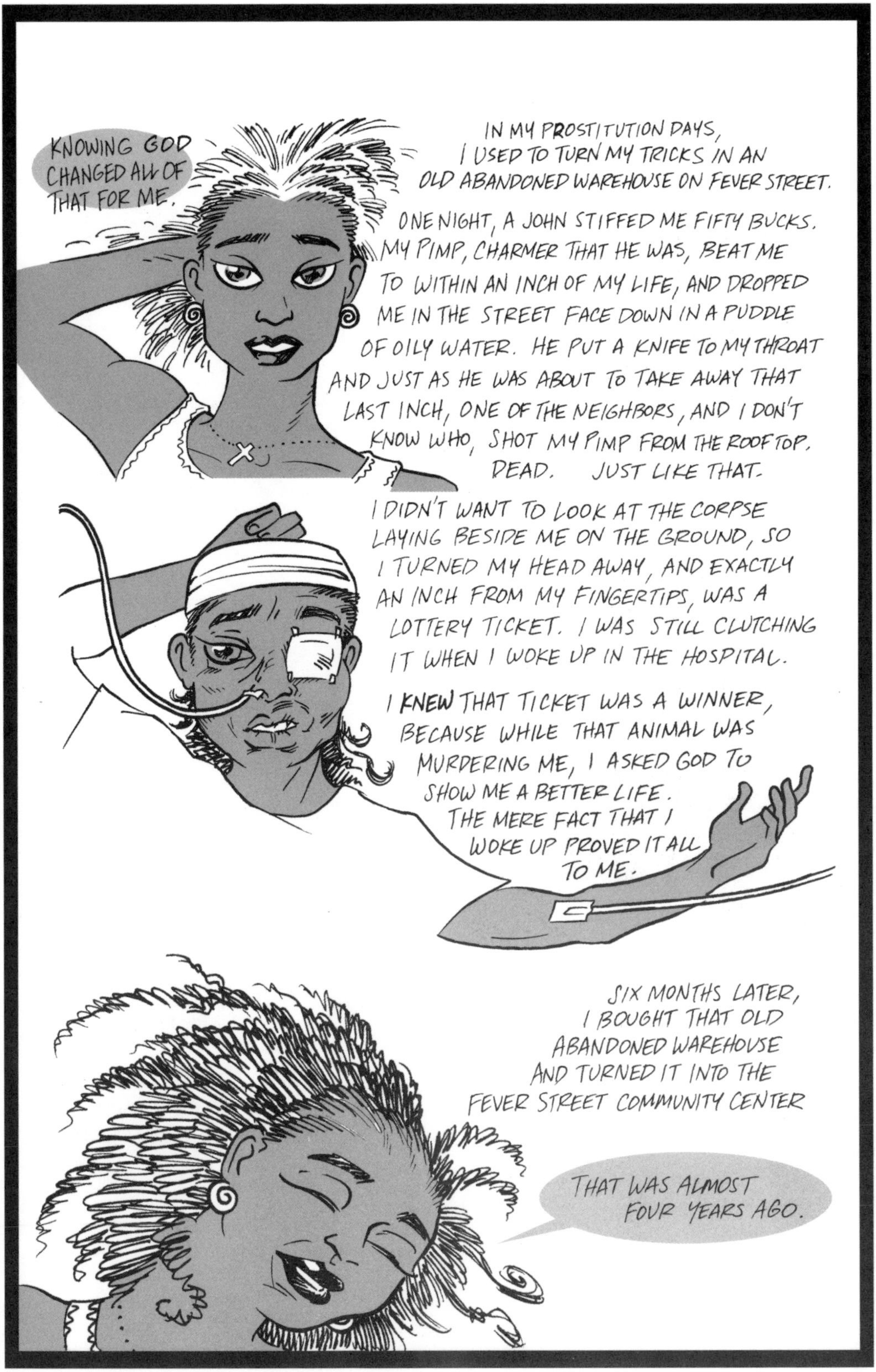
KNOWING GOD CHANGED ALL OF THAT FOR ME.
IN MY PROSTITUTION DAYS, I USED TO TURN MY TRICKS IN AN OLD ABANDONED WAREHOUSE ON FEVER STREET.
ONE NIGHT, A JOHN STIFFED ME FIFTY BUCKS. MY PIMP, CHARMER THAT HE WAS, BEAT ME TO WITHIN AN INCH OF MY LIFE, AND DROPPED ME IN THE STREET FACE DOWN IN A PUDDLE OF OILY WATER. HE PUT A KNIFE TO MY THROAT AND JUST AS HE WAS ABOUT TO TAKE AWAY THAT LAST INCH, ONE OF THE NEIGHBORS, AND I DON'T KNOW WHO, SHOT MY PIMP FROM THE ROOF TOP. DEAD. JUST LIKE THAT.
I DIDN'T WANT TO LOOK AT THE CORPSE LAYING BESIDE ME ON THE GROUND, SO I TURNED MY HEAD AWAY, AND EXACTLY AN INCH FROM MY FINGERTIPS, WAS A LOTTERY TICKET. I WAS STILL CLUTCHING IT WHEN I WOKE UP IN THE HOSPITAL.
I KNEW THAT TICKET WAS A WINNER, BECAUSE WHILE THAT ANIMAL WAS MURDERING ME, I ASKED GOD TO SHOW ME A BETTER LIFE. THE MERE FACT THAT I WOKE UP PROVED IT ALL TO ME.
SIX MONTHS LATER, I BOUGHT THAT OLD ABANDONED WAREHOUSE AND TURNED IT INTO THE FEVER STREET COMMUNITY CENTER
THAT WAS ALMOST FOUR YEARS AGO.

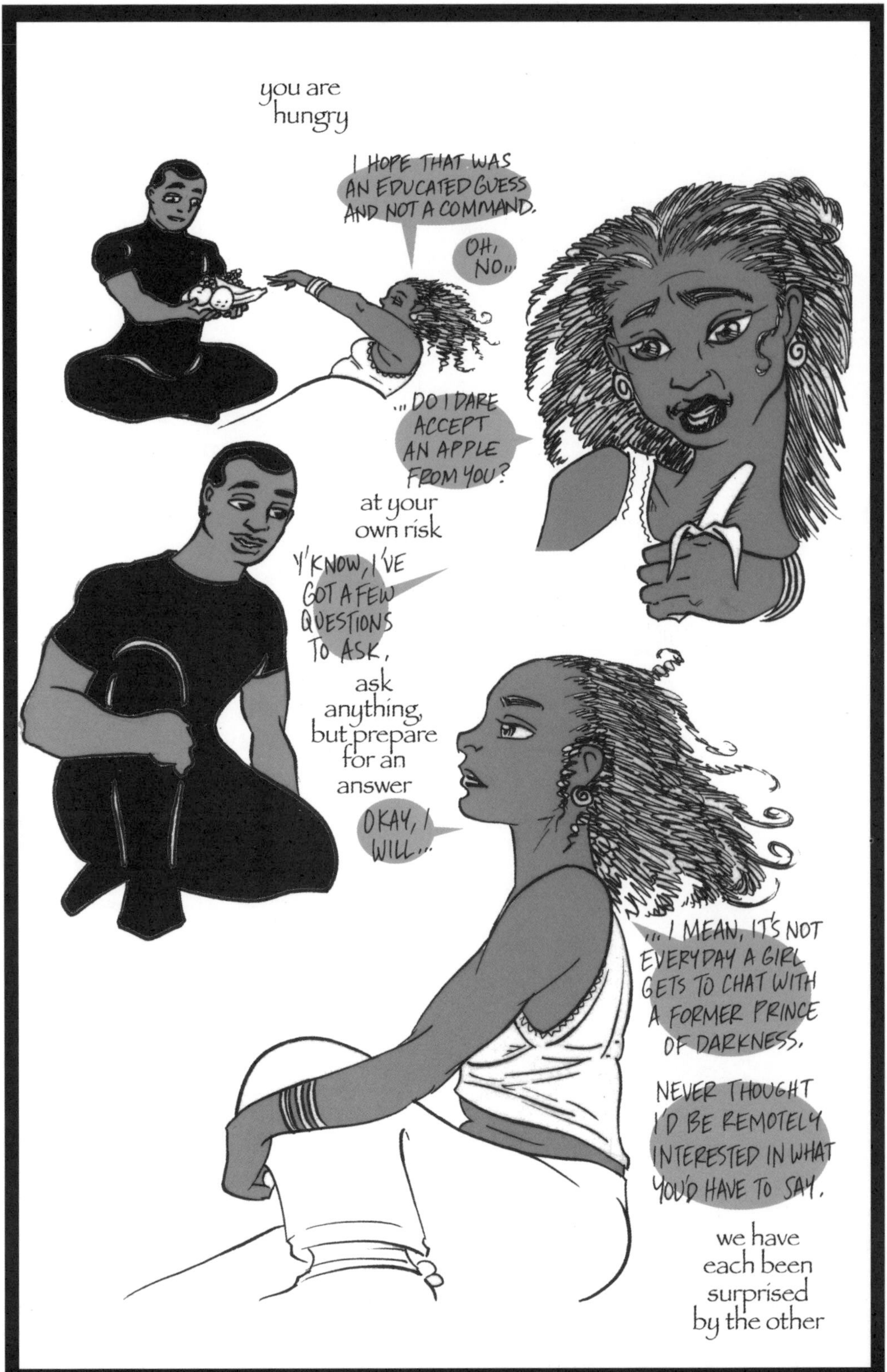
you are hungry
I HOPE THAT WAS AN EDUCATED GUESS AND NOT A COMMAND.
OH, NO...
...DO I DARE ACCEPT AN APPLE FROM YOU?
at your own risk
Y'KNOW, I'VE GOT A FEW QUESTIONS TO ASK,
ask anything, but prepare for an answer
OKAY, I WILL...
...I MEAN, IT'S NOT EVERYDAY A GIRL GETS TO CHAT WITH A FORMER PRINCE OF DARKNESS.
NEVER THOUGHT I'D BE REMOTELY INTERESTED IN WHAT YOU'D HAVE TO SAY.
we have each been surprised by the other

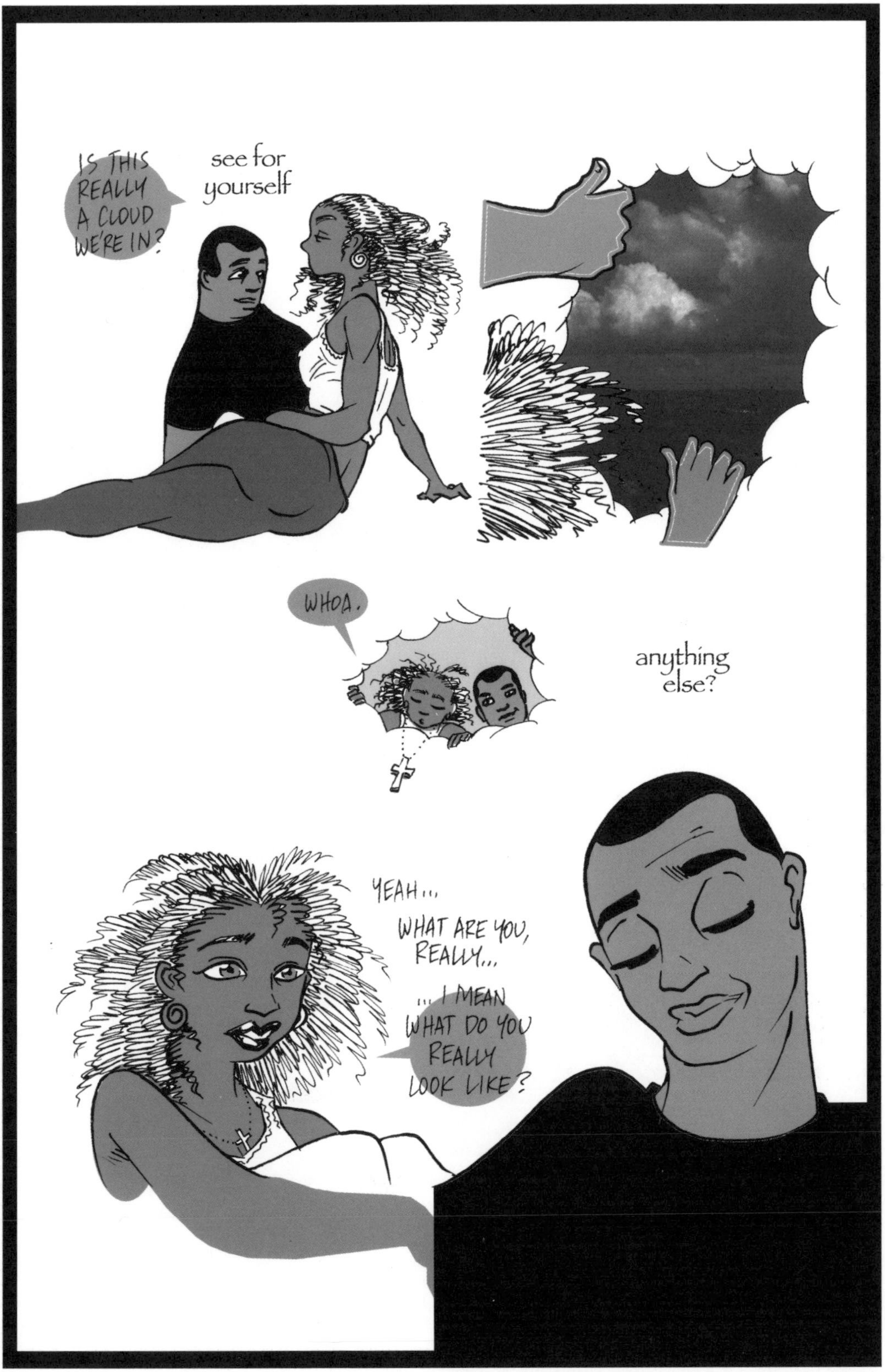
IS THIS REALLY A CLOUD WE'RE IN?
see for yourself
WHOA.
anything else?
YEAH...
WHAT ARE YOU, REALLY...
...I MEAN WHAT DO YOU REALLY LOOK LIKE?

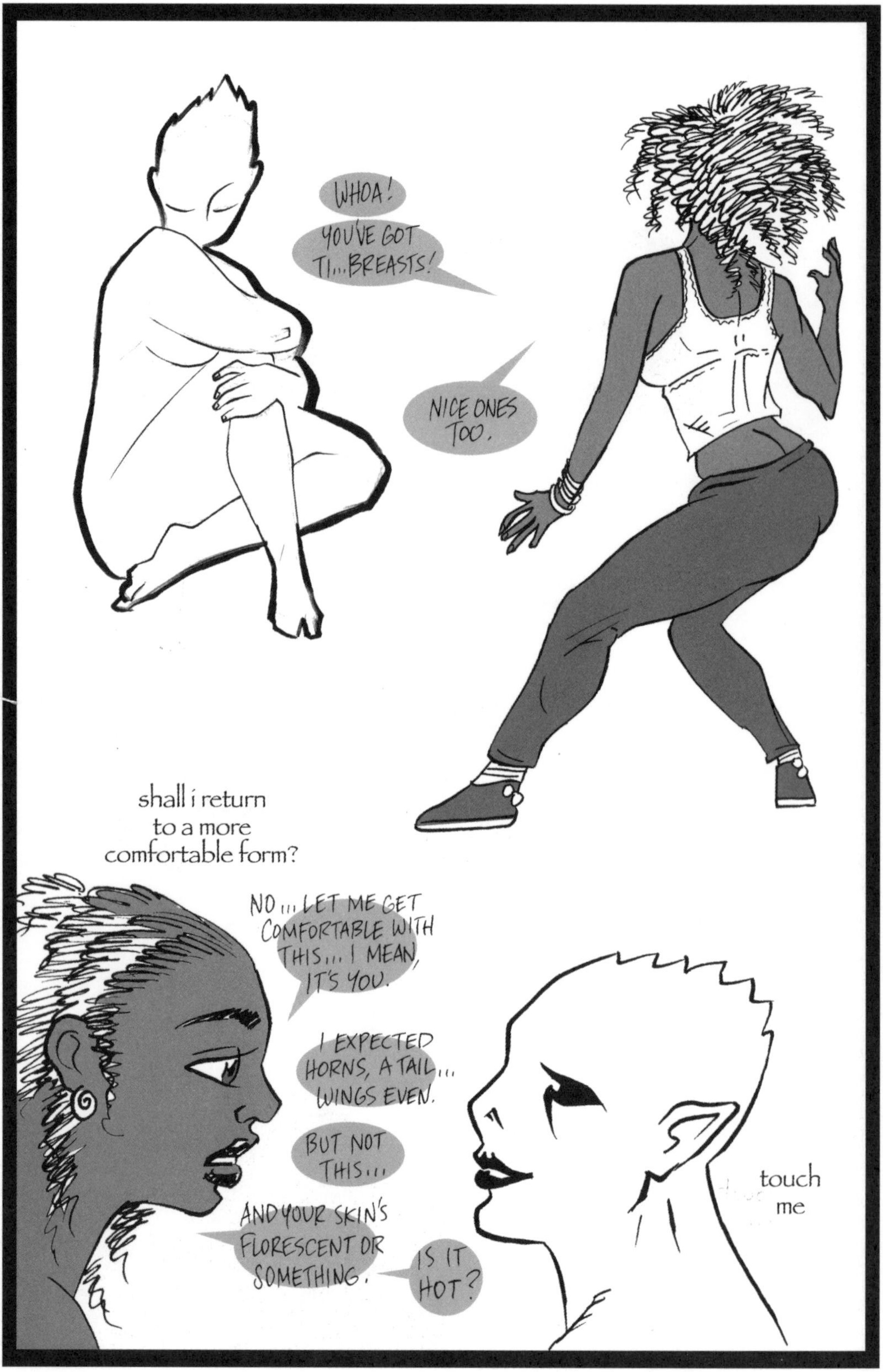
WHOA!
YOU'VE GOT TI... BREASTS!
NICE ONES TOO.
shall i return to a more comfortable form?
NO... LET ME GET COMFORTABLE WITH THIS... I MEAN, IT'S YOU.
I EXPECTED HORNS, A TAIL... WINGS EVEN.
BUT NOT THIS...
AND YOUR SKIN'S FLORESCENT OR SOMETHING.
IS IT HOT?
touch me

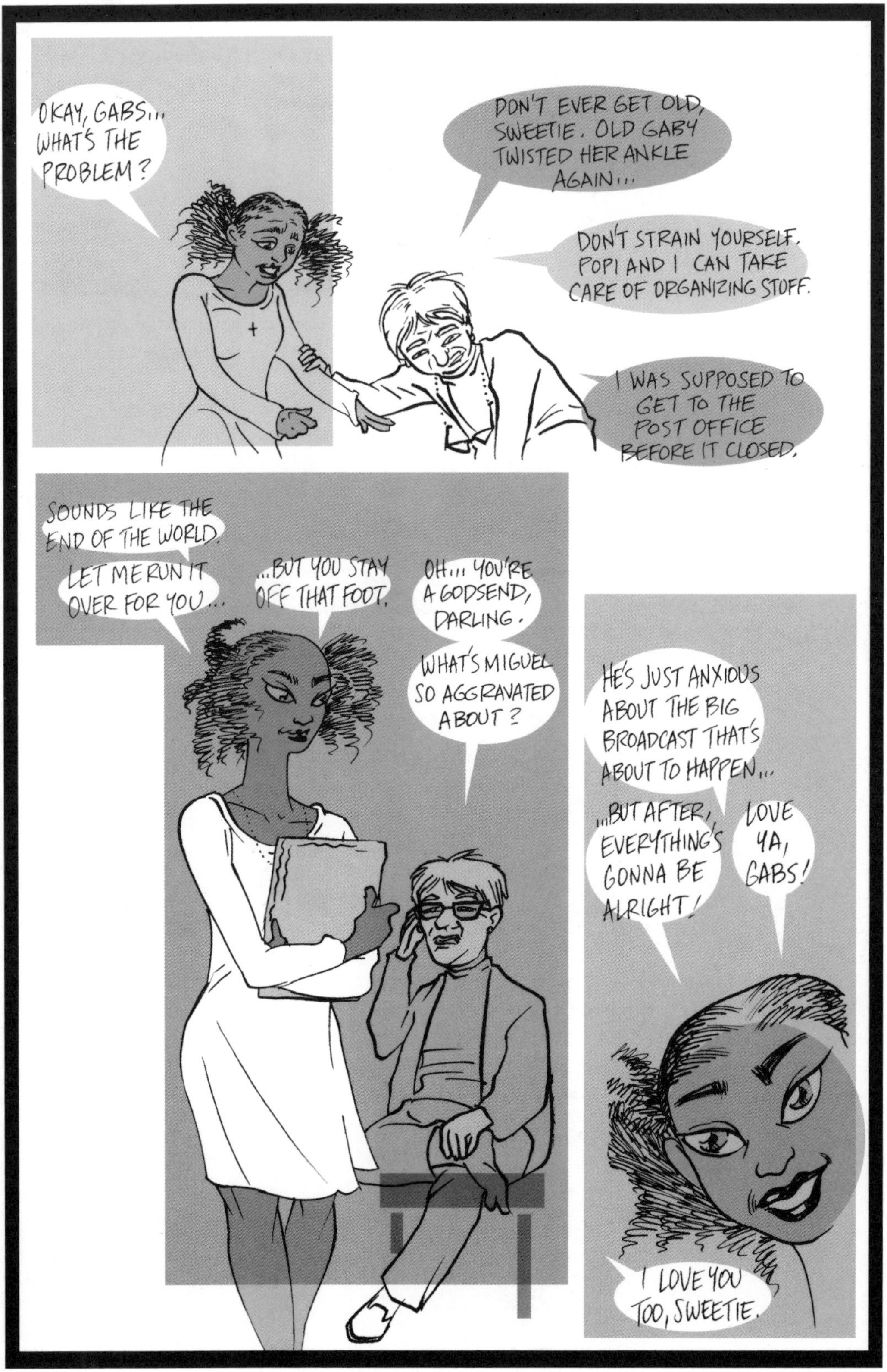
OKAY, GABS... WHAT'S THE PROBLEM?
DON'T EVER GET OLD, SWEETIE. OLD GABY TWISTED HER ANKLE AGAIN...
DON'T STRAIN YOURSELF. POPI AND I CAN TAKE CARE OF ORGANIZING STUFF.
I WAS SUPPOSED TO GET TO THE POST OFFICE BEFORE IT CLOSED.
SOUNDS LIKE THE END OF THE WORLD.
LET ME RUN IT OVER FOR YOU...
...BUT YOU STAY OFF THAT FOOT.
OH... YOU'RE A GODSEND, DARLING.
WHAT'S MIGUEL SO AGGRAVATED ABOUT?
HE'S JUST ANXIOUS ABOUT THE BIG BROADCAST THAT'S ABOUT TO HAPPEN...
...BUT AFTER, EVERYTHING'S GONNA BE ALRIGHT!
LOVE YA, GABS!
I LOVE YOU TOO, SWEETIE.

i, who am the angel, lucifer morningstar come to you with a message of hope

i, who was once the worst among you have come to see the error of my ways

you that know of me are doubtless aware of my misdeeds across time...
i am to blame for these things, and i am deeply sorry

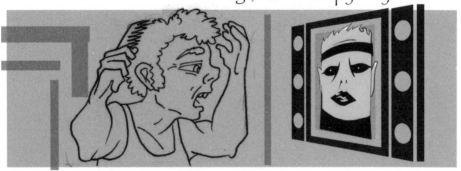

i beg for His mercy and pray that He, and you of this world, can find it in
your hearts to forgive me my trespasses, and believe that my soul can too
be saved by the everlasting love of God

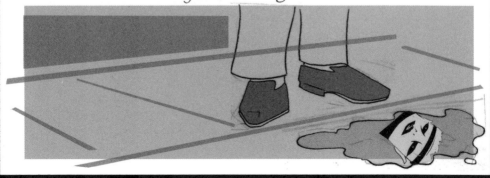

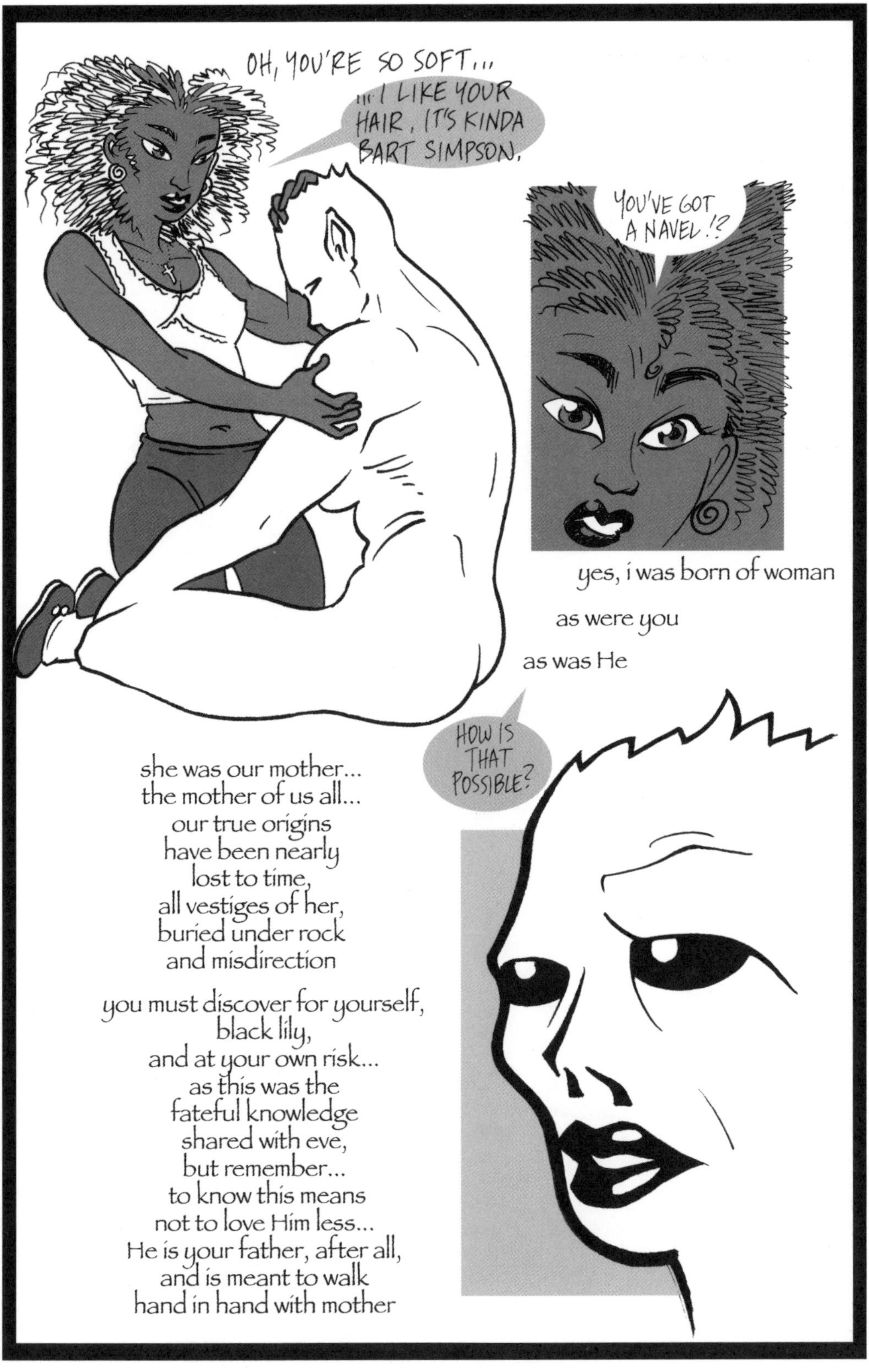
OH, YOU'RE SO SOFT...
...I LIKE YOUR HAIR, IT'S KINDA BART SIMPSON.
YOU'VE GOT A NAVEL!?
yes, i was born of woman
as were you
as was He
HOW IS THAT POSSIBLE?
she was our mother...
the mother of us all...
our true origins
have been nearly
lost to time,
all vestiges of her,
buried under rock
and misdirection
you must discover for yourself,
black lily,
and at your own risk...
as this was the
fateful knowledge
shared with eve,
but remember...
to know this means
not to love Him less...
He is your father, after all,
and is meant to walk
hand in hand with mother

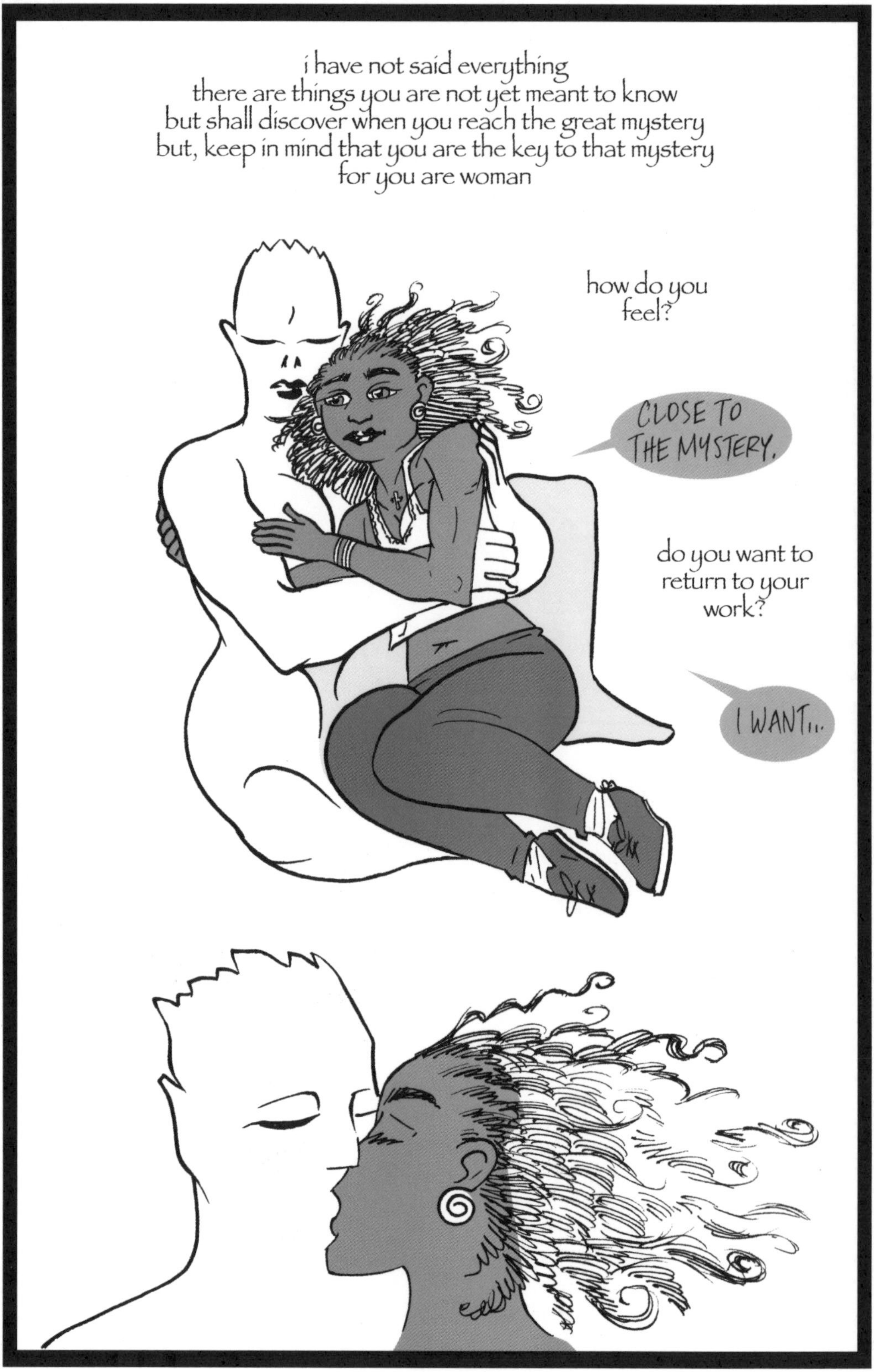
i have not said everything
there are things you are not yet meant to know
but shall discover when you reach the great mystery
but, keep in mind that you are the key to that mystery
for you are woman
how do you feel?
CLOSE TO THE MYSTERY.
do you want to return to your work?
I WANT...

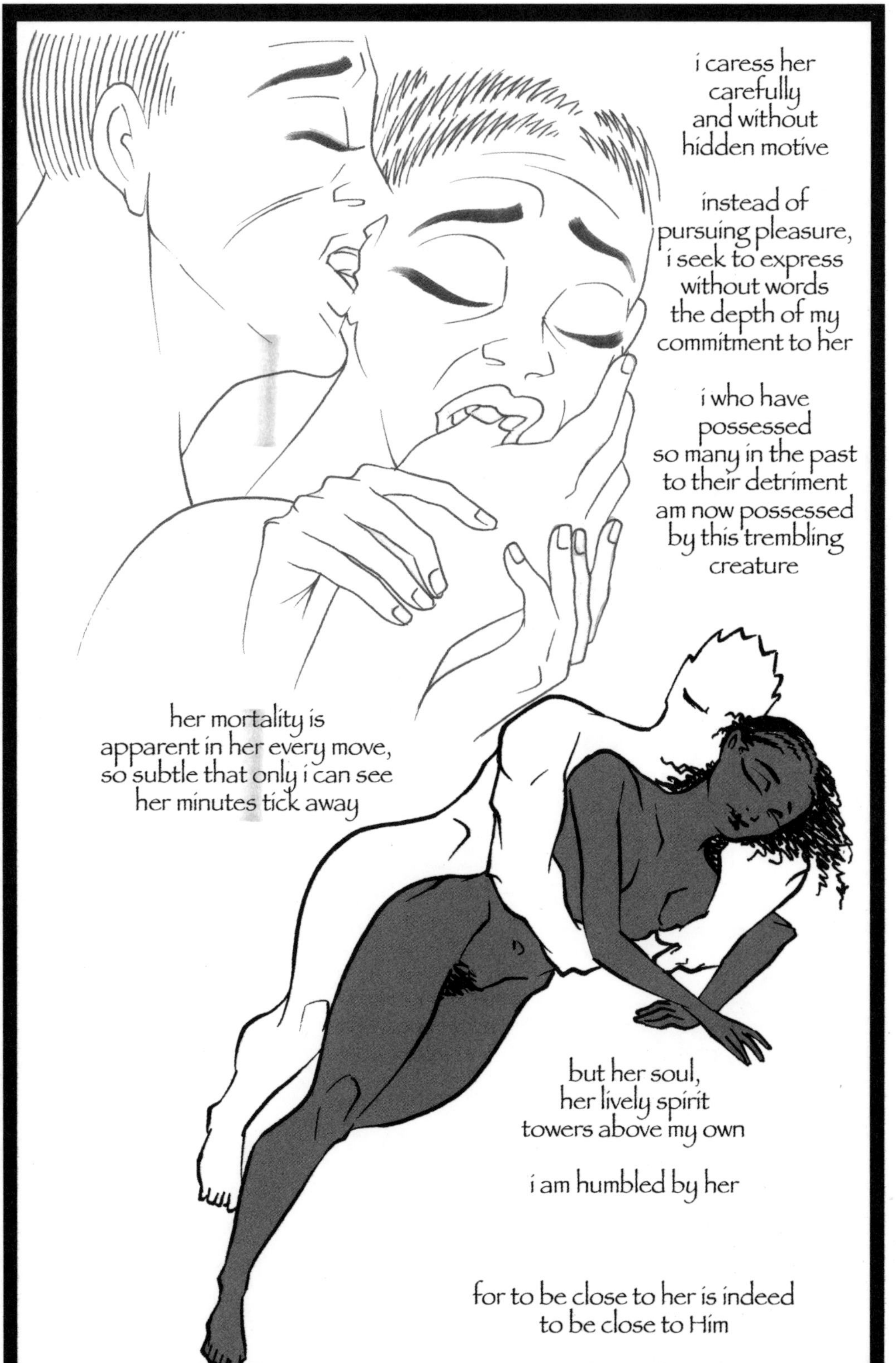
i caress her carefully and without hidden motive
instead of pursuing pleasure, i seek to express without words the depth of my commitment to her
i who have possessed so many in the past to their detriment am now possessed by this trembling creature
her mortality is apparent in her every move, so subtle that only i can see her minutes tick away
but her soul, her lively spirit towers above my own
i am humbled by her
for to be close to her is indeed to be close to Him

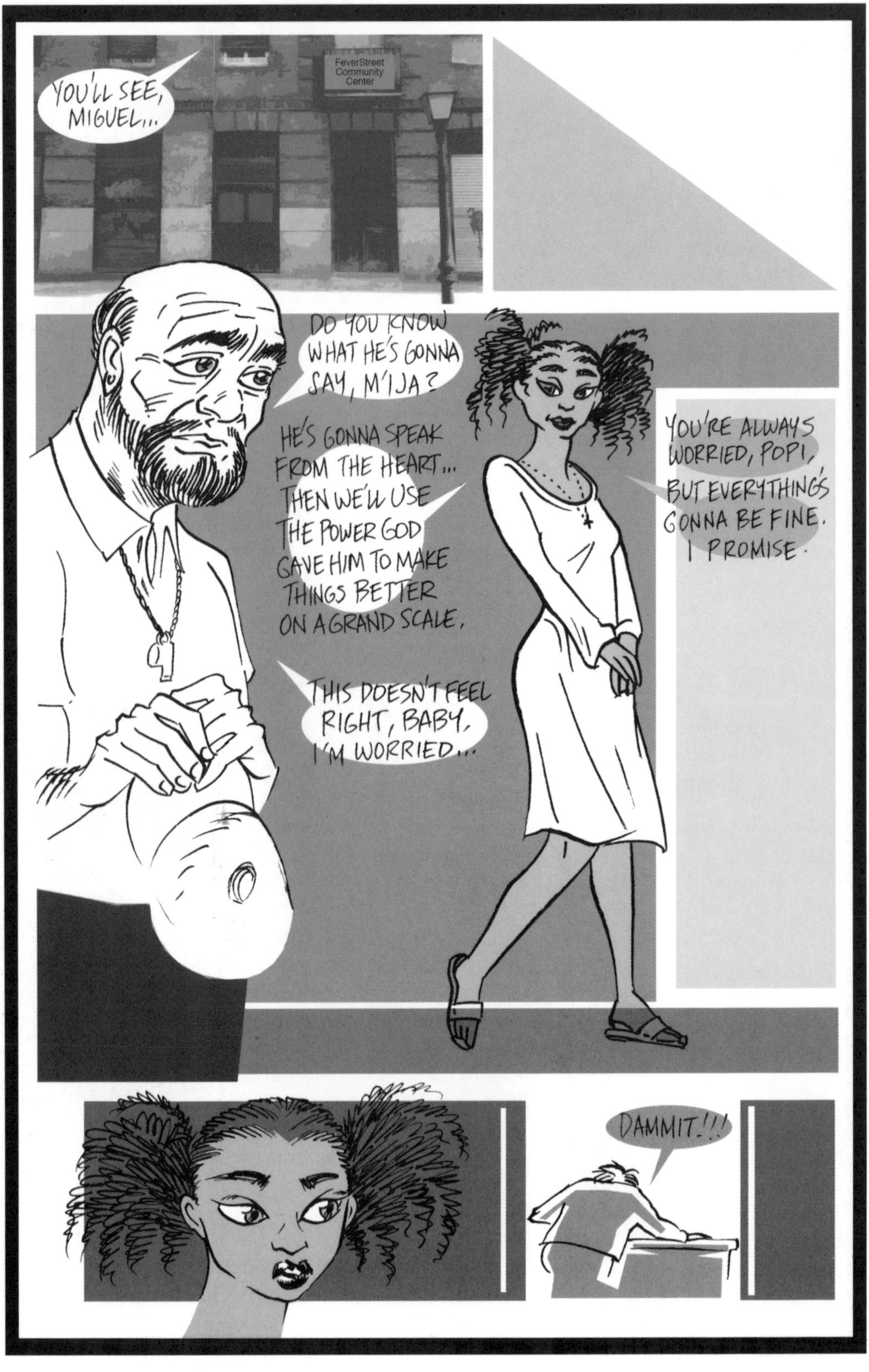
FeverStreet Community Center
YOU'LL SEE, MIGUEL...
DO YOU KNOW WHAT HE'S GONNA SAY, M'IJA?
HE'S GONNA SPEAK FROM THE HEART... THEN WE'LL USE THE POWER GOD GAVE HIM TO MAKE THINGS BETTER ON A GRAND SCALE.
YOU'RE ALWAYS WORRIED, POPI, BUT EVERYTHING'S GONNA BE FINE. I PROMISE.
THIS DOESN'T FEEL RIGHT, BABY. I'M WORRIED...
DAMMIT!!!

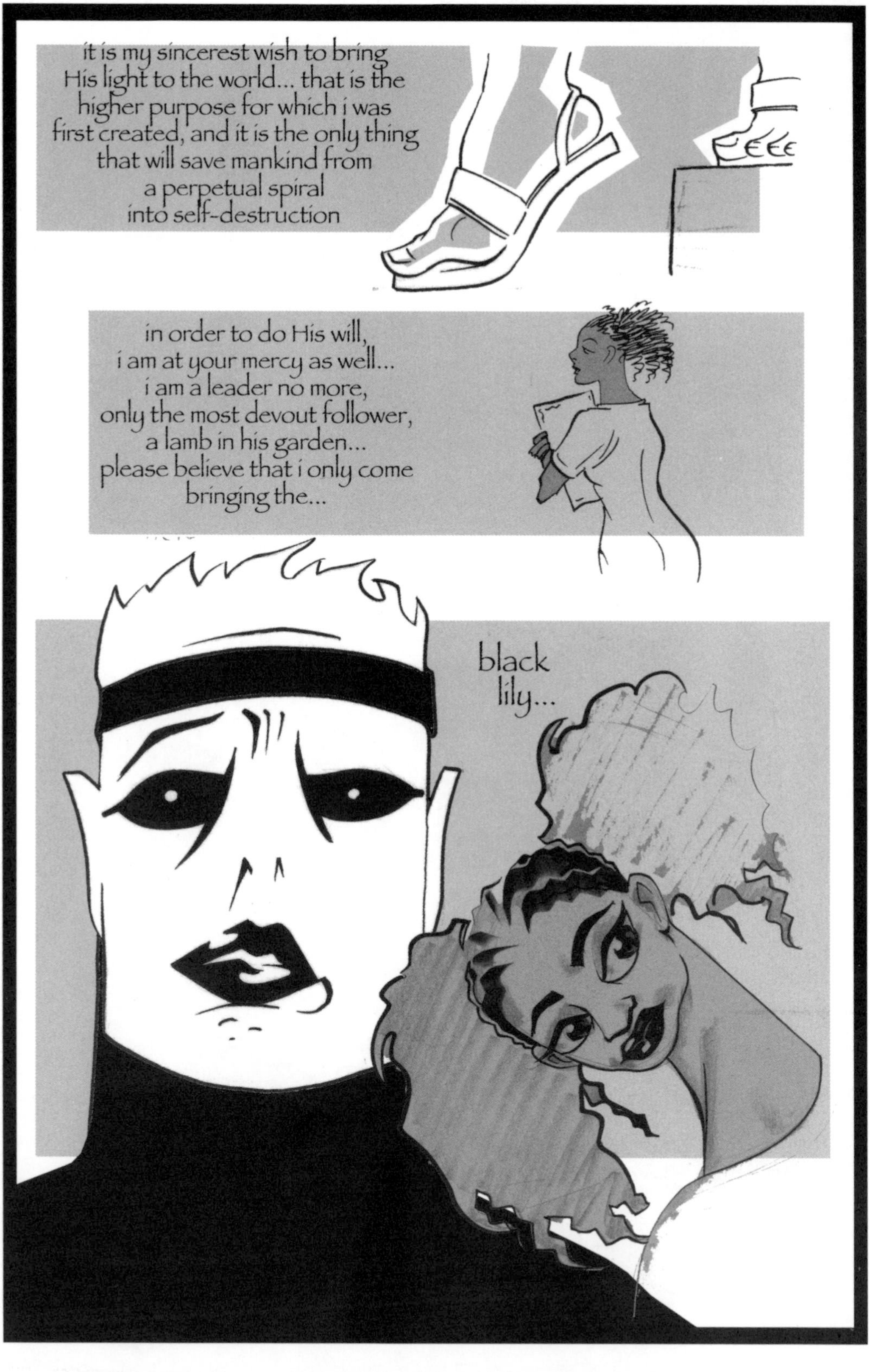
it is my sincerest wish to bring His light to the world... that is the higher purpose for which i was first created, and it is the only thing that will save mankind from a perpetual spiral into self-destruction
in order to do His will, i am at your mercy as well... i am a leader no more, only the most devout follower, a lamb in his garden... please believe that i only come bringing the...
black lily...

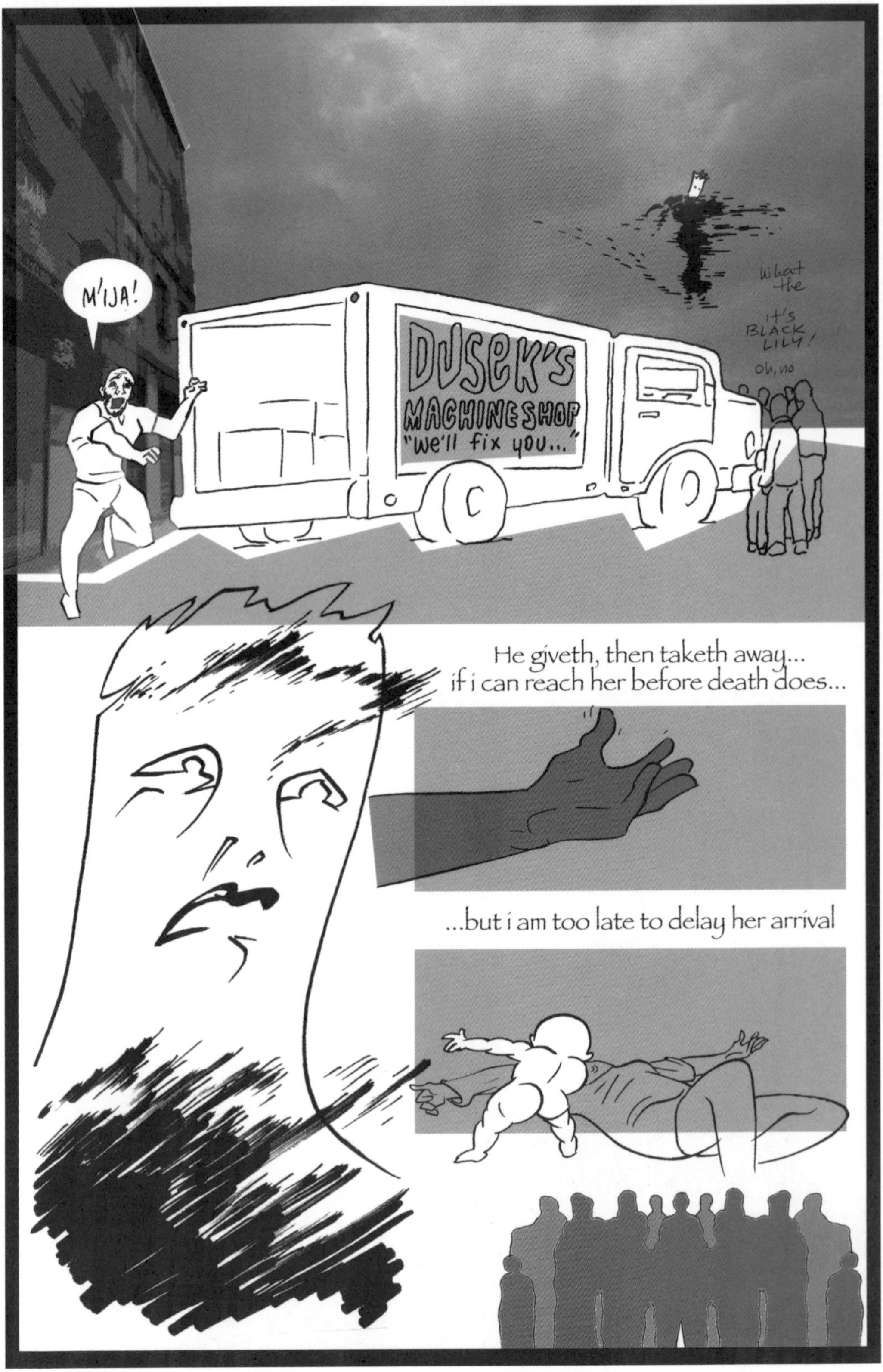
M'IJA!
DUSEK'S
MACHINE SHOP
"We'll fix you..."
What the
IT'S BLACK LILY!
Oh, no
He giveth, then taketh away...
if i can reach her before death does...
...but i am too late to delay her arrival

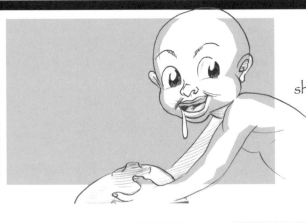

invisible to all,
death gorges herself
on vital fluids;
her thirst quickly sated,
she disappears, leaving behind
only a shell of the
angel of fever street

HELP!

THERE'S NO
DRIVER IN
THE TRUCK!

OH, MY...

MY BABY...
SWEET BABY.

IT WAS
AN ACT OF
GOD...

IS
SHE...

SLIPPED
OFF THE
JACK...

invisible to all,
and for only the slightest moment,
a thin spiral of light appears in the sky

fever street stands
before me transformed,
from what black lily made it,
into the center of
all suffering in the world

and who is to blame?

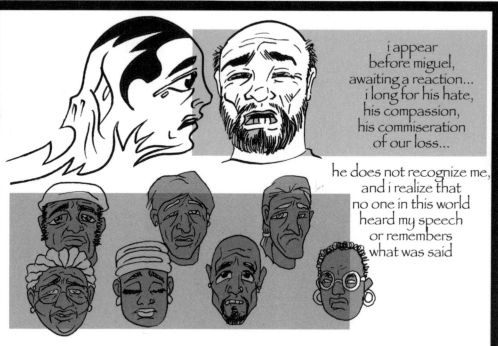

i appear before miguel, awaiting a reaction... i long for his hate, his compassion, his commiseration of our loss...

he does not recognize me, and i realize that no one in this world heard my speech or remembers what was said

i am Satan, the white hot weapon of apocalypse; my soul explodes with the fury of ages; i want to punish this puny world and all who dwell upon it

but, suddenly, all feeling deserts me

and i sit drained

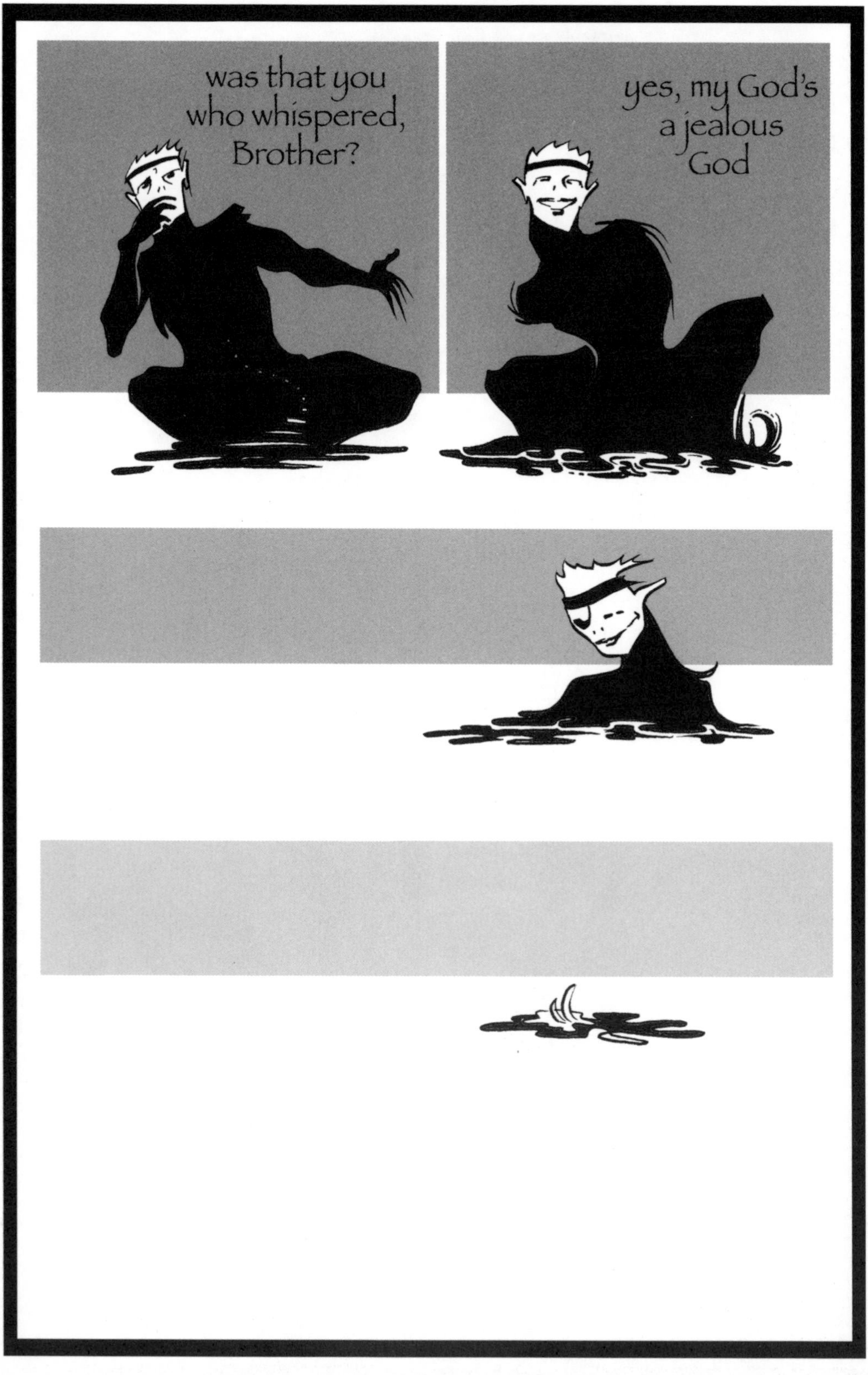
was that you who whispered, Brother?
yes, my God's a jealous God

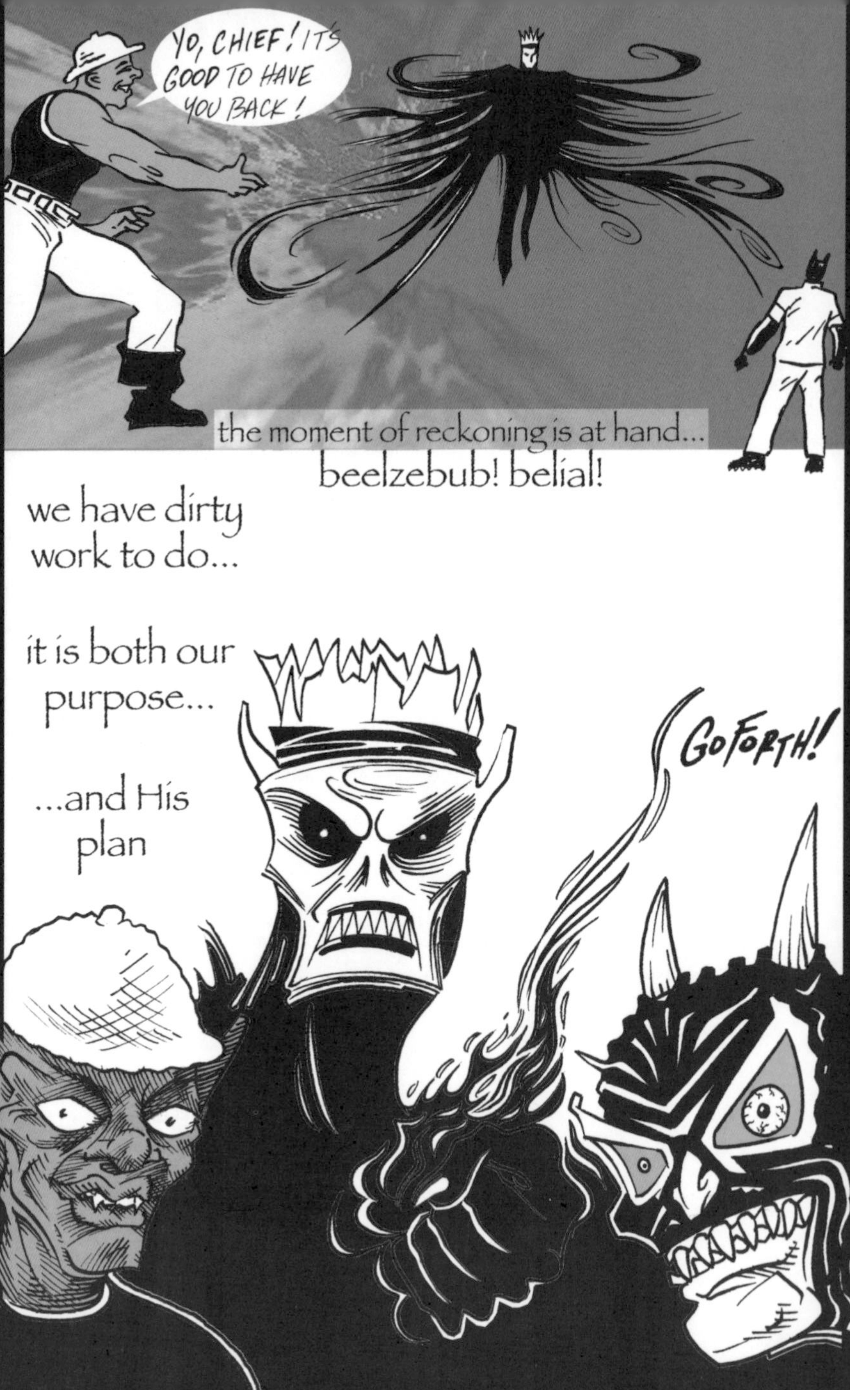
YO, CHIEF! IT'S GOOD TO HAVE YOU BACK!
the moment of reckoning is at hand...
beelzebub! belial!
we have dirty work to do...
it is both our purpose...
...and His plan
GO FORTH!

ha, ha, ha, ha, ha, ha

there is hope for all, but not for me
as i throw the curtains back

revealing
only
darkness,

and more
darkness

who among you will dare presume to speak to me of hell

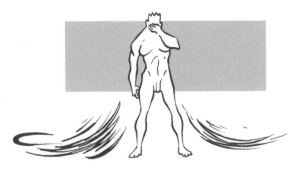

and who among you can possibly comprehend
what it means to dwell there

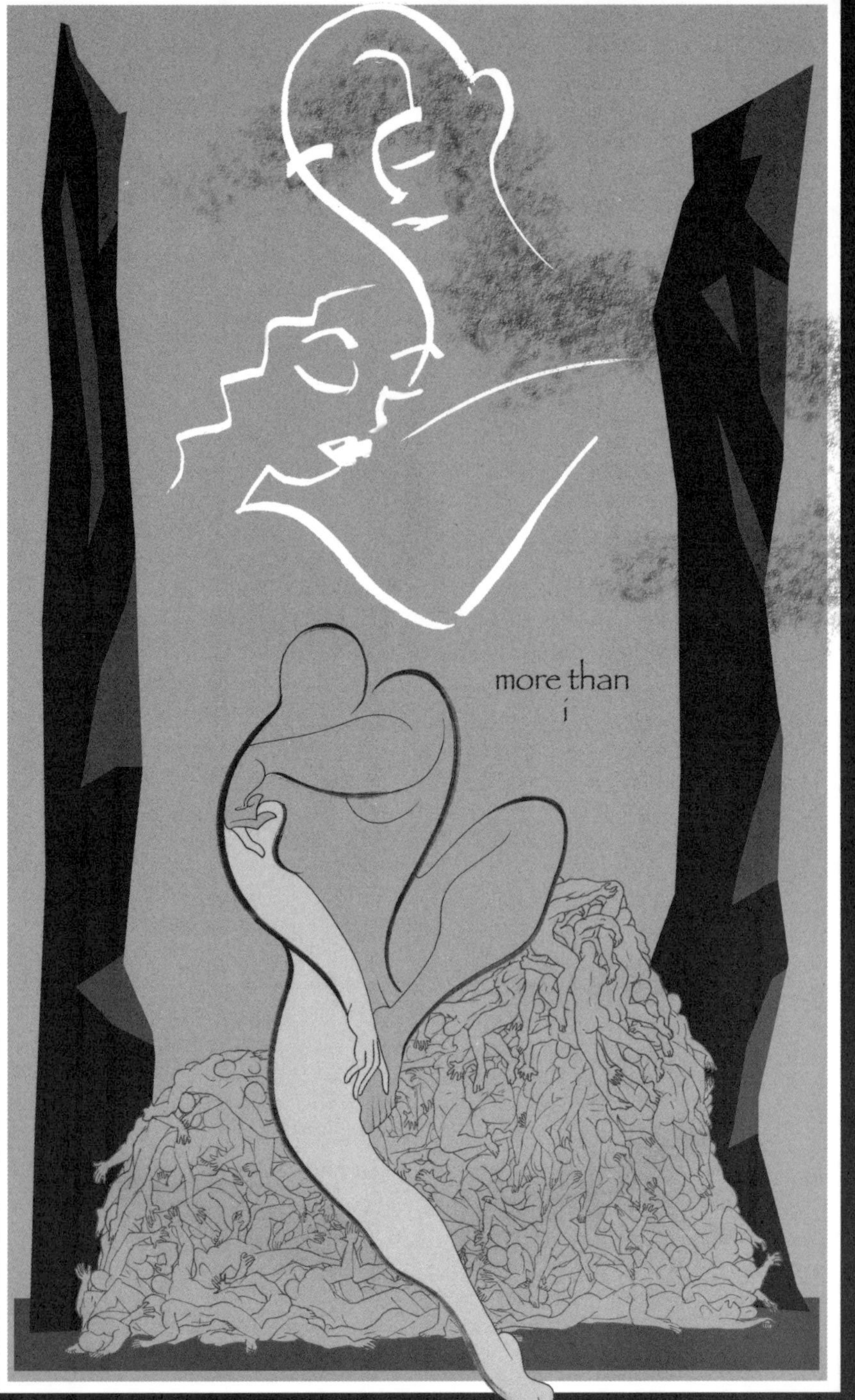
more than
i

lance tooks
would like
to thank:

terry, martin,
& the staff
@ n.b.m.

kevin. j. taylor,
geoff johnson,
doug hines,
titus thomas,
tonya smay,
gil giles,
steve johnson,
tom pomplun,
deb cowell,
jason little,
sean taggart,
randy duburke,
dr. muerte
& nurse jenny

this sculpture of the
fallen angel lucifer
in madrid's retiro park
is said to be the only
statue of the devil
in a public park
in the world

these photos
were taken by
professor sergio calvo

gracias sergio y pilar, sergio y
sonia, esther y juanda, lalo y
mercedes, patri y alejandro,
mama y papa y el rorro

thanks to mom & dad,
uncle george and anne,
kimmy, seanie & major tom,
eric & stef,
harry & mary, kristi & maria,
olivia & sakai, santiago & sofia,
tanya mckinnon
dominic, ed sted, chris, pete
& mikey taliban

frank armitage is dedicated
respectfully to john carpenter

que te
quiero,
sunijoe

"...the fault,
dear brutus,
lies not
in our stars,
but in
ourselves..."

-shakespeare,
felix unger &
my pop

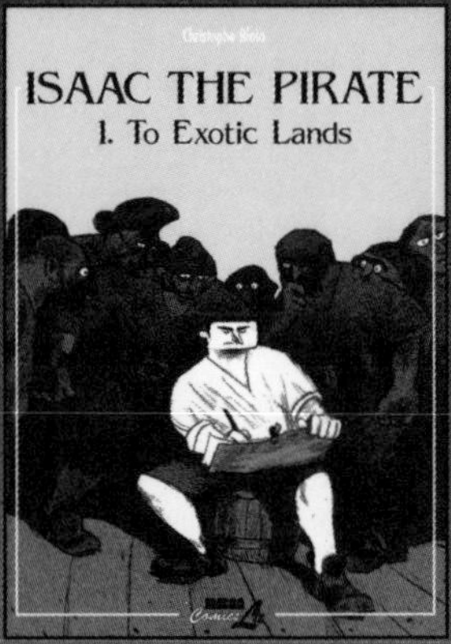
ISAAC THE PIRATE
1. To Exotic Lands

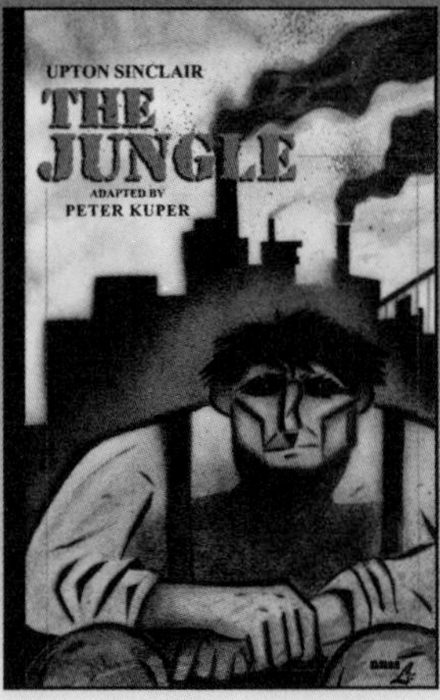
UPTON SINCLAIR
THE JUNGLE
ADAPTED BY
PETER KUPER

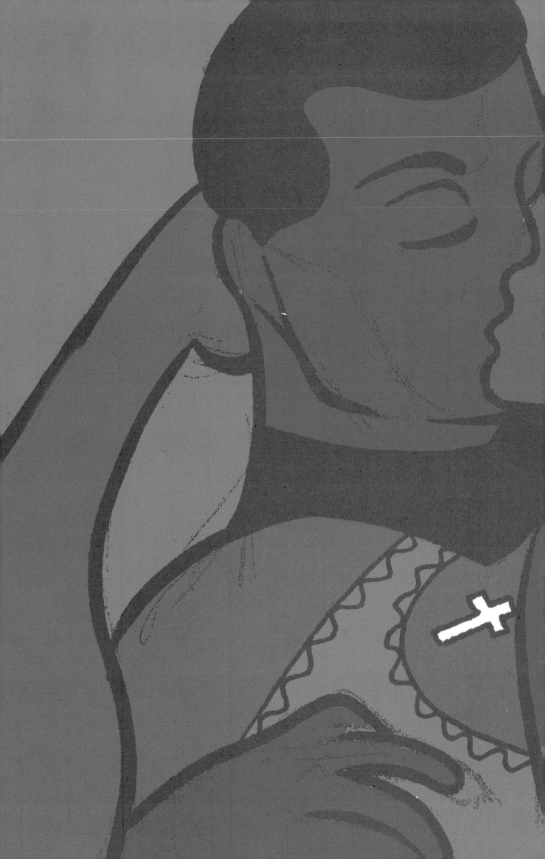